BILLIE PIPER

BILLIE PIPER
THE BIOGRAPHY

NEIL SIMPSON

JOHN BLAKE

Published by John Blake Publishing Ltd,
3 Bramber Court, 2 Bramber Road,
London W14 9PB, UK

www.blake.co.uk

First published in paperback in 2006

ISBN 1 84454 318 8
ISBN 978 1 84454 318 2

British Library Cataloguing-in-Publication Data:

A catalogue record for this book is available from the
British Library.

Design by www.envydesign.co.uk

Printed in Great Britain by Bookmarque

1 3 5 7 9 10 8 6 4 2

Papers used by John Blake Publishing are natural, recyclable products made
from wood grown in sustainable forests. The manufacturing processes conform
to the environmental regulations of the country of origin.

CONTENTS

1
MEET ROSE

FIGHTING DALEKS, SLITHEENS and Autons was one thing, but at 7.15pm on Saturday, 26 March 2005, Billie Piper knew she was facing the biggest enemy of all – Ant and Dec and the Saturday night television audience.

Billie had put everything she had into the role of Rose Tyler, Doctor Who's newest and noisiest assistant. During the filming, there had been eight months of pre-dawn calls and midnight finishes. Afterwards, there had been a seemingly endless round of publicity interviews and photo sessions. In between, Billie's marriage had ended and her whole world had been uprooted and moved down the M4 to the BBC's state-of-the-art studios in Cardiff.

Finally, more than a year after first auditioning for the *Doctor Who* role, she was going to find out if it had all been worthwhile.

Adding to the pressure was the fact that Billie was very much the star of the first episode of this new series. There was intense interest in Christopher Eccleston as the ninth Doctor. But this very first show was called 'Rose', and Billie dominated the screen from the start. Writer Russell T Davies had defied *Doctor Who* convention by telling this first story largely from Rose's point of view. Viewers who had forgotten who the Doctor was and what he did would learn through her eyes. It was up to Billie to make Britain fall back in love with a show which hadn't been on our screens for more than 15 years.

As she paced around her house in north London, Billie was well aware that success was far from guaranteed. Her face was on billboards, newspaper adverts and magazine covers across the country in one of the BBC's most expensive publicity campaigns. But she couldn't get a recent article from the *Times* out of her mind, an article that predicted a humiliating flop for the new show. 'Pre-transmission market research suggests that the BBC is heading for a £10 million disaster. Pollsters found that viewers thought *Doctor Who* was a niche series for science-fiction geeks,' was the essence of the report. The big screen remake of *Thunderbirds* had just bombed in the cinemas. Were sci-fi revivals really so far out of fashion?

Billie looked around her house. She had spent the last few months joking with the BBC producers that she wanted a Dalek to put in her hall – and they had said she wouldn't be able to have one while the show was on air.

If tonight's audience reaction was as bad as the critics feared, then Billie knew she might need to clear some space pretty quickly.

'If you're an alien, how come you sound like you're from the North?' That was Billie's favourite line from the first show, delivered as Rose tries to understand exactly who the Doctor is and what he is doing in her world. Billie asked the question with a style that set the tone for the whole series. Irreverent, real, contemporary. But would enough people see and hear it?

David Beckham, of all people, was the star guest on *Ant and Dec's Saturday Night Takeaway* that night. 'Wouldn't more people prefer to watch him rather than watch me get together with a mysterious 900-year-old man?' Billie admits she probably asked herself the question a million times as the transmission time got ever closer.

As it turned out, they didn't. The new *Doctor Who* trounced Ant, Dec and David Beckham in the ratings. At its peak, some 10.6 million were watching and the figures would beat the BBC's expectations for the remainder of the 13-week run. Despite the last-minute fears, the audiences and the critics were almost universally positive. Everyone liked the show, and suddenly everyone loved Billie Piper.

Her ability as an actress was what shattered expectations. After dominating the eponymous first episode, she seemed to go from strength to strength as the series progressed. Episodes such as 'Father's Day', where Billie's Rose re-lived the death of her father, were emotionally wrenching. Others, such as 'The End of the World' and 'The Unquiet Dead' were simply stunning, exciting and terrifying in equal measure. In each of them, Billie didn't just hold her own, she frequently carried the show. What made the series work was the fact that almost everyone could enjoy it, young or old, first-time viewer or long-standing fan. Billie was an immediate hit with the younger, new audiences. But she also won some serious fans among the old-timers — including former Doctor Who Sylvester McCoy.

He had won the lead role in 1987 with Sophie Aldred playing his teenage assistant Ace. He said he liked everything about the revived show and, while he said he knew next to nothing about her, he said he loved Billie most of all. 'Billie Piper as Rose is awesome, just wonderful to watch. She's real, she's here, she's now; she makes you believe the most unbelievable things. Apparently, she has had quite a turbulent personal life, but I don't read the tabloids. All I know is that she is so right for the part. Russell T Davies says she is going to be our next great Hollywood export and, on the basis of this performance, I can well believe it.'

For Billie, the praise was extraordinarily important, because it came from a fellow professional who wasn't overloaded with preconceptions of who she was and what she had done. She was still just 22 years old, but sometimes it felt as if she had lived as many lives as her fictional Doctor. And sometimes the baggage from those lives threatened to stop her in her tracks.

It was a long time since she had won her first acting job in a commercial at just seven years old. It was a long time since she had packed her suitcase as a 12-year-old, said goodbye to her parents, her sisters and her baby brother and gone to stage school in London. It was a long time since she had been at Number One in the pop charts — on three separate occasions. It was a long time since she had got married, wearing flip-flops, in Las Vegas. And on a good day, it even felt like a long time since her marriage had ended and her new life as a single woman had begun.

On that late spring Saturday night in 2005, all that was forgotten as the first episode of *Doctor Who* came to its end. In the final seconds, just before the famous music started to play, more than ten million people would see Billie run, in slow motion, into the TARDIS. She was running because, after an agonising decision, Rose had picked a life of adventure and excitement over one of mundane routine. Billie herself had made that choice many years ago. Her life had taken her to some amazing highs and some terrible lows. She had done so many things, learned so many lessons… and she didn't regret a single day.

2
THE GIRL FROM SWINDON

SEVEN-YEAR-OLD Billie Piper was admiring her new clothes as she flew backwards and forwards on a makeshift swing. But she wasn't in the park, at school or on holiday; she was in a photographic studio in Central London… at work.

A huge crew was buzzing about her as everyone got ready for the next take. Today, no one can remember quite why the breakfast cereal company had decided Billie should be suspended in mid-air to advertise the product. But she can remember every other tiny detail about her first day in the spotlight. At the start of the day, some of the adults on the set had thought the little girl had been shaking with nerves. In reality, Billie says she was shaking with excitement. At just seven years old, she was exactly where she wanted to be, and she didn't want to forget a single thing. 'I was wearing brand new Marks

& Spencer hot pants and some crazy peach leotard. I just loved it, all of it. I remember leaving London afterwards and feeling like crying. Even though it is only 60 miles up the road from Swindon, it's a completely different way of life. And after doing the commercial there, I knew for certain that it existed and I was desperate to have it, to taste it, again.'

It was strong stuff from someone so young. But then Billie always had been a girl with a mission. A girl in a hurry.

As a sign of things to come, *The Kids from Fame* were at Number One in the album charts on 22 September 1982 when Leanne Paul Piper was born at the Princess Margaret Hospital in Swindon. Paul was her dad's name, and no one in the family seemed to think it was an unusual name to give to a girl as well – not least because Billie's grandmother Margaret had always been known as Mickey. Funnily enough, it was the name Leanne that turned out to be a problem.

Once Mandy and Paul took their first daughter home, they decided she didn't look anything like a Leanne. Out of nowhere, they thought she looked like a Billie, so they took advantage of the opportunity all parents get to change their minds and had her birth certificate updated – simultaneously correcting the fact that their little girl had been registered as a boy by a clerk who had been misled by her middle name. Even with the right paperwork, it is no surprise that Billie took a while getting used to being different.

'I got so much stick from the other kids at school about my names and when I was little I would really resent my parents for it. Now I wouldn't want to be called anything else. I've got really different names and I love that,' she says.

The Piper family started to grow quickly after Billie's arrival and, by the time younger sisters Harley and Ellie and a younger brother Charlie had arrived, mum Mandy was a full-time housewife. Dad Paul owned his own building firm and Billie says she learned her ferocious work ethic by watching him throw everything he had at creating and expanding his business.

For her part, Billie's play always had a purpose. She was endlessly pretending she was a grown-up actress, dancer or singer, always trying to persuade her friends to join her in the latest theatre company, dance or singing troupe she had invented to work for. Her grandmother, a former dressmaker, remembers being constantly on hand to run up costumes for the performances. And when Billie wasn't having fun with her gran, she was dreaming other dreams with her grandfather. As an ex-railway worker, he qualified for a free family railcard and Billie was constantly begging him to take her on trips to London where she could breathe in the atmosphere of the big city. Even the dullest streets, the most anonymous houses, the ugliest buildings thrilled her. She would sit on the train gazing out the windows as they approached Paddington Station, desperately trying to imagine who lived there, what they did and where they were going in life.

Looking back, Billie says she has no idea where this love of London began. She didn't know why she thought it was so exotic, or why it figured so highly in all her dreams. 'I was bored of being a child really early and I couldn't wait to grow up. I was so ambitious, though I don't know where that came from. I just always knew I wanted to be famous and I wasn't going to let anything stop me. And that meant I had to get out of Swindon and go to London,' she said. 'I used to play with Ouija boards a lot with my friends. I would ask questions like, "Do you think I will be an actress when I get older?" Then I would manoeuvre the board so it looked like it was spelling out "Yes!"'

Before then, Billie had plenty more advertising work to do. Her constant play-acting as a child had persuaded her mother to take her along to a local drama class where they had found details of a child modelling agency. Mandy was told that most kids who sign up don't find much work, and many find the auditions terrifying. Billie proved to be different on both counts. She thrived on the auditions, getting a buzz simply by being in a creative, competitive environment — and she got work straight away. After her first job promoting cereal, she won a singing role in a commercial for a new range of yoghurt-based shampoos and starred in an American advert for a soft drink. Other children may well have been terrified by the occasion, and frozen by the pressure. Billie was simply thrilled to be out of her Swindon comfort zone and aiming for the stars.

'It's funny because I've not got some sort of tragic, childhood tale,' she says of her early obsession with escape. 'We didn't have a lot of money but neither did we wear the same shoes for three years or stuff like that. My parents are solid, lovely people, but I just wanted more all the time. I was desperate to be an adult, to do stuff on my own, to see things to get out of Swindon. I knew that if I stayed, I would end up really resenting my friends and my relationships.'

Years later, Billie reckons she can see it all more clearly. 'I still get nostalgic when I hear a song that reminds me of my childhood, of sitting in a car park eating a hamburger with my parents or something like that. But I knew I just didn't want to do that for ever. I didn't want to be there. I wanted to be in London, or America. And I wanted to work. My dad always had such an amazing work ethic and I got that from him. Work was always something that I wanted, even as a very young child.'

When she wasn't able to audition or win advertising jobs, Billie was just as keen on local talent shows – and she says she prayed every night that she would one day get the chance to be a professional actress or entertainer. The Pipers used to go on caravan trips around the country and Billie would always end up singing, dancing or reciting poetry on stage in any holiday centre or village hall they discovered, drinking in the applause and the sheer excitement of performing.

Family birthdays were another favourite of Billie's – especially big ones held in pubs or halls where Billie could serenade the birthday boy or girl, increasing in confidence and range every year. Her mum Mandy, who had once dreamed herself of being a dancer or a singer, was keen to help her daughter make the most of her talents. And with Paul playing the double bass at home, there was plenty of creativity in the Piper household to inspire Billie to do just that.

Drama, not surprisingly, was Billie's favourite subject at school. She was also keen to sign up for as many theatre classes as possible both during and outside school hours. Her other big strength was that she always seemed ready to take advice and learn new skills. She did modelling courses one summer not because she wanted to be a model, but because she thought it might help her perform as an actress. The teachers at the local Tanwood Dance School where Billie had started attending classes aged eight said she was one of the keenest youngsters they had ever seen – rarely if ever missing or even being late for a class.

Desperate to cram as much into her life as possible, Billie also auditioned for, and won a place at, the hugely prestigious Sixth Sense Theatre Company in the town, a professional theatre company which focused on performances for and with young people.

At Bradon Forest Comprehensive, she was soon attracting the attention of drama teacher David Calder as well. Already a girl in a hurry, he was on the point of casting her in a production of *Charlie and the Chocolate Factory* when Billie dropped a bombshell. She was leaving

Swindon and going to school in London on her own. She had been at Bradon Forest for less than three terms.

The London connection happened because teachers at the Sixth Sense Theatre Company had told Billie about what they thought was the best theatre school in the country. It was the Sylvia Young Theatre School, a so-called 'celebrity factory' based in an old church building just off Marylebone High Street in central London. The moment she heard about it, Billie wanted to be there. And the more she learned about it, the more determined she was to make her dream come true. 'I wanted to act every day, not just once a week or at an after-school class. I wanted to live surrounded by music and the Arts. At that age, most people only see acting as a hobby, but I already knew I wanted it to be more than that. I knew I wanted it to be my life.'

So she planned her escape with military precision. 'I went to my parents with a list of all the reasons why I wanted to go to stage school and just said, "This is what I want to do with my life," and I had an answer, information, or something to say, to every objection they could possibly have raised.' She was just 11 years old.

In London, the Sylvia Young Theatre School had a fantastic history – and a fearsome reputation. It had been set up by Sylvia Ruffelle in the early 1970s after her daughters wanted to put on an act to raise funds for a new swimming pool in Wanstead, East London. Sylvia got the community organised, helped put on the show then carried on offering weekly drama classes in a community centre on the local housing estate. The group put on more than 50 shows in its first year and took on the name The Young 'Uns. 'I had so many people calling up asking for "Mrs Young 'Uns" that I decided it should be called Sylvia Young,' Sylvia says. When the membership hit 90 — including soon-to-be *EastEnder* Nick Berry — the group started to be seen as a feeder route for West End shows, whose producers came round looking for young talent. It was also too big for its old home so, in 1981, Sylvia opened a full-time school in Drury Lane, the heart of London's theatre land. When the school's lease expired, it was the matron, Letitia Dean's mother, who found the premises in Marylebone where Billie went for her first audition in 1993.

As she and her mother walked through the courtyard and into the building, they were immediately aware of the calibre of the school's students. Photographs and names of former pupils were everywhere. And it many ways, they were a roll call of popular culture. When Billie arrived, Spice Girl Emma Bunton was just leaving, while All Saints stars Melanie Blatt and Nicole and Natalie Appleton were other recent graduates (and Billie would end up being a year ahead of another big music name — Amy Winehouse).

Among the actors, early student Nick Berry had been followed by the likes of Samantha Janus, Letitia Dean, Dean Gaffney, Denise Van Outen and Danniella Westbrook, plus a host of company members at the Royal National Theatre, the Royal Shakespeare

Company and the English and Scottish National Operas. Billie got the message loud and clear – if you want to make it in the acting world, you need to be at the Sylvia Young Theatre School. But would she get in?

The school has around 150 pupils, aged between 9 and 16. Around 24 new children are admitted each year – and in Billie's day, more than 1,000 applied. At that time, auditions brought 25 children together at a time, with no guarantee that any would be offered a place. But Sylvia sat in on each session to make sure she knew exactly what was happening. 'I watch for that spark, that certain something. It can be as simple as when a child smiles at you during an audition and makes you want to smile back. It goes beyond ability. I remember my notes on one girl said: "She's not very good, but I want her here." Fame is such a chancey thing, it takes you by surprise and you can never really predict who will make it.'

After her gruelling auditions and interview sessions, Billie was one of the students who caught Sylvia's attention. She wasn't just offered a place, she had also won a vital half-scholarship which meant her parents could afford the private fees which already topped £4,500 a year.

Back in Swindon, the first person Billie told outside the family was her drama teacher David Calder. The second, pretty much, was a reporter from the local evening paper. It was the 12-year-old's first taste of celebrity and, at this point, she quite liked it. 'I am really excited as I have always wanted to be an actress. This is the first big break for me,' she told the reporter who had come round to see her at school. It was hardly 'Hold the Front Page' sort of stuff, but the article, and the accompanying photograph of Billie and her classmates, went in the family's cuttings file. It would be the first of very, very many more.

Taking up her place at Sylvia Young did mean a lot of growing up for Billie. For a start, she was stepping into the unknown. 'I had only just moved to my new secondary school and had gone though the stage of making all new friends so it was hard to leave them and have to start all over again where I didn't know anybody. But I wanted it so badly and I knew that, if I didn't take the opportunity, I would regret it.'

The next point to consider was where she would live during term time. The distance involved meant she couldn't stay at home and she ultimately moved in with her great aunt and uncle in Barnes, south-west London and travelled to school every day by train and tube.

To counteract all the hard work, long days and intense competition at Sylvia Young, pupils say there is a supportive 'family' atmosphere at the school. And for youngsters such as Billie, who had moved away from home to attend, that was vitally important. 'Sylvia was always warm and supportive. The atmosphere she created was great, a real family environment,' says former pupil Samantha Janus. 'This school makes you very independent because you realise that, if you want to do well, you have to do it yourself. And Sylvia is brilliant. She'll always listen to you if you've ever got a problem,' says recent graduate and *Grange Hill* actress Charlotte McDonagh.

That said, the pressure was always on and you had to be on your toes – as Emma Bunton admitted at the height of her Spice Girls fame. 'I have performed in front of royalty and heads of state, but I was most nervous when Sylvia came to watch me at Wembley. I was worried whether she would think I was any good,' she said.

Unlike some performing arts schools and the whole *Kids from Fame* image, the focus at Sylvia Young is on drama rather than dance, and normal academic schoolwork is far from ignored. In Billie's day, as it is today, the school has a traditional academic headmaster. At the time, Billie's was Colin Townsend, whose aim was to get as many GCSE passes as possible. From Monday to Wednesday, the pupils all wear standard uniforms of blazers and black-and-red ties and follow a normal school curriculum. The long-term average is 85 per cent of pupils achieving five or more A–C grades, double the national average, it is all the more impressive as they are achieved in three days rather than five. People who visit the school comment that on the three academic days there is one key difference between its classrooms and those of an average comprehensive. At Sylvia Young, it appears, classrooms are full of pupils with their hands up. Everyone seems bright, confident, articulate and keen to prove themselves.

Of course, it was the remaining two days of the week

that Billie lived for. On Thursdays and Fridays the dress code changed. You head to class in loose black trousers and Sylvia Young School T-shirts or unitards. All the classes on those two days are in drama, dancing or singing. The energy is everywhere, the enthusiasm is infectious and the ambition unmistakable. Sylvia herself agrees she is ruthlessly keen for her kids to succeed, but she somehow manages to keep a sense of perspective about the industry she is propelling them towards. 'Is it a sausage factory for famous people?' she was asked of her school recently. 'I suppose it is. But they are individually made sausages. I don't think this is just a fame school, even though I know every child who comes here wants to be famous. In their last year, I tell them about fame's downside, about the pressures of it all. At the end of it, I ask them if they still want to be famous and they all say "yes".'

What Billie was also finding was that the school was no place for slouches. Sylvia famously expelled her own daughter, Frances, for being disruptive (mother and daughter have since been reconciled and Frances has gone on to become a Tony Award–winning actress). For Billie, hard work was already second nature. And she found it easy to keep her head down and avoid any of the potential bitchiness of such a competitive environment. Looking back, she says she owes everything to her time at the Marylebone school and doesn't regret a single moment she spent there. But she is also prepared to admit that it wasn't all dancing on the tables and rapturous end-of-term performances. 'It was hard work and it was lonely at times,' she says. 'It's also hard because you go from a place where you are the only person with your sort of ambition to a place where everyone has it. It could be a tough old life. But I could hardly complain because it was exactly what I wanted. I couldn't sit around thinking, "God, I am so tired, I've only had six hours sleep." Instead, I just thought, "More! More singing! More dancing! More cabaret!" I was so starry-eyed and so happy. I just couldn't wait to get to bed at the end of every day so I could get back up again and do it all again. And I was so ambitious, all the time.'

What Billie also thrived on was the breadth of the Sylvia Young approach. The promise the school made to casting agents and potential employers was that its best graduates could cope in almost any entertainment environment – actors who could sing; singers who could act; dancers who could do all three. The idea was to produce one-stop shops for the industry and make sure the school would be recognised as the first port of call for everything from extras to all-star casting.

Billie, her face lighting up with enthusiasm the moment she walked into an audition, was ready to take full advantage. Like every other Sylvia Young student, she was automatically signed up to the in-house agency, Young 'Uns, and latterly its adult equivalent, Rossmore. Billie got results, just as she had done back in Swindon. One of her first and most exciting roles was on *EastEnders*. She was only an extra, a face in a crowd tucked away most of the time in the audience of the fashion show Patsy Palmer's Bianca put on at the Walford Community Centre. But being at the Elstree Studios, seeing the stars Billie adored and getting a real look at the behind-the-scenes working of a major soap was an incredible thrill. Like every other professional job Billie won, this one left her wanting more.

Over the next few years, she also got a part in ITV's Saturday morning children's show *Scratchy and Co* where she played Posh Spice in a spoof of the 'Who Do You Think You Are?' Spice Girls video. 'It was great fun because I adore the Spice Girls. And how did I play Victoria? I just sucked my cheeks in and struck a few silly modelling poses,' is how she remembers it.

And there were two even bigger experiences to come, moments which would confirm Billie's long-standing belief that she wanted to be an actress. The two jobs were both on major film sets, the first for *Evita*, and the second for the theatrical romp *The Leading Man*.

Being on the same set as Madonna in *Evita* was a huge thrill for Billie. *The Immaculate Conception* was the first album Billie ever bought and she said 'Vogue' was one of her favourite songs of all time. Once more, Billie was simply in a crowd scene (though there is a big close-up of her face at a dinner table), and again the whole learning curve of being on a huge Hollywood-funded film was incredibly important to her. As, of course, was the chance to do some serious star-gazing. 'I didn't get to speak to Madonna but just to be near her was amazing.

I was nearly crying I was so happy. My big ambition now is to perform with her,' Billie said afterwards – acting her age, for once in her life.

In *The Leading Man*, Billie's duties as an uncredited extra left her able to mingle with a similarly stellar British and international cast including Jon Bon Jovi, Thandie Newton, Barry Humphries, Diana Quick and Patricia Hodge. Unlike *Evita*, the film pretty much sank without trace on its release and Billie and her family had to scour the screen to see even a flash of her face in the crowd scenes. But it was one more item to go on Billie's theatrical CV; one more step in the direction of a full-time acting career.

As Billie knuckled down in the first half of her school weeks, trying to decide which GCSEs to take, she was looking equally far ahead to her drama days. As the years went by, she was very aware of how competitive the atmosphere at Sylvia Young was becoming. So how could she edge ahead of all her classmates and beat them to the top? The girl who had made her first commercial at seven was determined never to fall behind. She didn't just want to make it, she wanted to make it soon.

With this in mind, she realised that the more work she did, the more opportunities she could create. So when Billie saw an advert looking for the new face of *Smash Hits!* magazine, she put herself forward straight away. She was 15 and she had no idea just how quickly her life was going to change.

3
'POP!'

'OK, BILLIE, ARE you ready?'

Billie nodded, smiled and put yet another piece of pink bubble gum in her mouth. Nearly 1,000 people had replied to the *Smash Hits!* advert but Billie had got the job. And filming the adverts was proving to be quite a challenge. Her task today was to run towards the camera, blow and burst a bubble with her gum and then shout, 'Pop!' While in theory it might sound easy, anyone who has ever tried to get a bubble big and round enough and burst it without getting gum all over their face can attest that it was trickier than it seemed. Hence the growing pile of gum wrappers building up around Billie's feet as the number of takes hit double figures.

Billie, getting ready to run at the camera one more time, was blissfully happy, however. She was in her element and she was ready to do as many takes as the creative team required. She looked around as the photographer and his lighting crew prepared for action. A hair-stylist rushed forward to push back her fringe, while a make-up artist was waiting off camera with a touch-up brush. It was eight years since Billie had filmed her first commercial, but she certainly hadn't lost any of her early excitement.

The *Smash Hits!* executives watching in the wings of the central London studio were equally relaxed about the number of takes it needed to get the advert in the bag. They were utterly convinced that Billie was the face that would rebuild their magazine's fortunes. They knew that when the adverts were completed they would get the perfect message across.

'We wanted someone who would typify the reader,' said editor Gavin Reeve. 'Bright, intelligent, sparky, a bit of attitude, a bit of an edge. We wanted the cool girl in the class. And lots of girls came in — wannabe acting girls with pushy mums, girls who obviously weren't ever going to be anything. But Billie had real character. She was by far the best.'

Billie had also got noticed by arriving at her audition straight from school. Dozens of the other hopeful models had all arrived dressed up to the nines, the creative team said. Billie was in her school uniform but she still managed to persuade the professionals that she had what it took. Margaret Hefferman, the advertising brand manager specifically charged with relaunching the magazine, was enthusiastic from the start. 'Billie screened amazingly well on camera. And she was multi-talented – she had to sing, dance and act all at the same time for this job and she knew the pressure was on in the audition. She handled it like a professional and was our obvious choice.'

Heading back to Barnes that evening, Billie was fizzing with excitement over a job well done. She was already thinking of how to phrase it on her resumé and she was desperately looking forward to seeing the first print and television ads get a showing. She was also hoping that some of the people she had met in the studio might have been impressed enough to put her name forward for other castings in the future.

As it turned out, they didn't need to. A record executive called Hugh Goldsmith was soon to see one of the stills from the campaign on the cover of *Music Week* as news of the pop magazine's relaunch broke. Hugh was the controller of Innocent Records, a new offshoot of the massive Virgin label, and he was looking for a teenage singer to fill the gap being left by the Spice Girls. He had very specific ideas about the kind of girl he was looking for. And when he looked at the sparky kid with the bubble gum, he thought he had found her.

Innocent's marketing manager, John Paveley, was told to find out more. 'It was all a bit of a gamble but we tracked Billie down through the magazine and her school and put her in a studio to find out if she could sing,' he says. With an ever-protective Sylvia Young waiting in the wings, the record executives were all blown away.

'Billie recorded a cover of an R Kelly song and it was

fantastic,' says Paveley. 'I don't think there is a thing the girl can't do. I've seen a holiday video of her when she was eight, dancing to Madonna, and even that was brilliant.'

The video wasn't enough to convince everyone about Billie's talents, though. So after proving her range with several more songs, she was put through a tough dance audition as well. It was an unexpected, intimidating challenge for the 15-year-old, who hadn't expected to do anything but sing that day. But she couldn't have cared less. She got on to the tiny stage, did as many routines as she could think of and passed her test. The record company wanted her.

Hugh Goldsmith was particularly impressed. And as one of the industry's most respected A&R men, he knew exactly what he was looking for and what would sell. 'Billie's vocals were absolutely beautiful. She had a great tone — she sounded a little bit black — and she had soul. I was instantly taken with her. She had that impossible-to-define quality that you look for in a star. A very strong look, very strong features. Almost like a beautiful Manga cartoon character. All that and a huge smile, utterly charming, just a delightful girl.' He felt, instinctively, that Billie was what he was looking for.

But for a while it looked as if he might lose her. Amazingly enough, he was told there was a chance that Billie could turn him down and make him start his search all over again. 'When I first spoke to Sylvia about Billie, she said that her talents were, in order, acting, dancing and singing,' remembers Hugh. 'Sylvia said she was actually a little disappointed that a singing opportunity had come along and that, because of it, Billie might not ever pursue her acting career.'

The thought that someone might say no to a pop career had hardly occurred to any of the Innocent bosses before. In normal circumstances, they were used to the exact opposite – being deluged with letters, demo tapes and assorted pleas from wannabe stars with differing degrees of talent. Conventional wisdom had it that it was the record company executives who picked the potential stars, not the other way round. But conventional wisdom was to be turned on its head when 15-year-old Billie Piper came into the frame.

She left the record bosses speechless by proving to be an extraordinarily tough negotiator. She echoed Sylvia Young's words and told the executives that her key ambition was to be an actress. 'Singing seems exciting,' they remember her telling them, with extraordinary understatement. But she said she wanted an absolute assurance that it wouldn't take her too far off course from her ultimate goal of acting. 'A career in music can open doors for you,' they promised, astounded that they were suddenly being forced to sell themselves to the teenager. 'Filming pop videos is a form of acting,' they told her, increasingly desperate. 'This is an opportunity you just can't miss.'

With hindsight, the teenage Billie was on amazingly shaky ground. At any point, the top brass at Innocent could have told her that they would rather find someone less opinionated, less confident and much more malleable. But in the back of their minds, none of them seemed able to forget that surprisingly soulful voice. They were looking into those big, beautiful brown eyes... at that open, excited look with its perfect combination of confidence and vulnerability. A battle of nerves had begun in the Innocent offices. Billie was no longer just another conveyor belt pop star they could make money from then throw away. She was someone they desperately wanted to win and she had raised a point they were equally keen to prove. By holding back and staying true to her long-held ambitions, Billie had unwittingly turned herself into a must-sign artist. It was the age of girl power and Billie was embodying it before a note had been sung. If she stayed this strong, the company was convinced she could be a star like no other.

Throughout her singing career, many critics would dismiss Billie as just another manufactured pop act. A puppet, singing other people's songs and following other people's rules, they said. The reality was very different, as the Innocent bosses had discovered in their board room that day in 1998.

After deciding to take the gamble, Billie also proved herself to be one of the hardest grafters in the business. Her dad, Paul, had to co-sign her contracts and, as a successful businessman, he was determined to read through all of them and get advice on anything he wasn't clear about. But Billie just wanted him to hurry up and sign. She was ready to get started. She wanted to work.

The exact cost of launching a new recording artist is hard to pin down. So many departments are involved; so many bills from production to publicity need to be paid. But industry estimates in 1998 said that Innocent was prepared to spend up to £1 million making and marketing their new teen star. The stakes were high and there were no guarantees that even this would produce a chart-topping artist. But what was certain was that it was never going to be an easy ride. Billie and her parents were told just how much she was going to have to do in the next six months and beyond. The company wanted a big return on its investment. And her life was going to change for ever as she tried to produce it.

The first thing Billie had to do was say goodbye to everyone at the Sylvia Young School – the second school Billie had left early in the past three years. Her last day came at the end of the spring term and created an enormous stir among her schoolmates. Yes, it was a stage school where every student dreamed of making it big and winning a fantastic entertainment contract. But that didn't make it any less exciting when one of them actually did so. 'The news about Billie spread round the school in about 30 seconds and, as you can imagine, there was a real mix of excitement and envy,' said Jack Bevan, who was in the year below Billie. 'She was doing what we all wanted to do and I think, if it did anything, it made us all even more ambitious about doing the same the following term.'

After the Easter break, Billie was allocated a private

tutor and her new management company were told to try and find her around three spare hours a day for study. Meanwhile, Hugh Goldsmith was trying to find the perfect song to launch her career. He had liked the R Kelly and Prodigy songs she had tackled in her early auditions but he wanted her back in the studio as soon as possible to see how she could handle a whole range of other styles and sounds. He also had something else he wanted her to try – the four-strong writing team of Dion Rambo, Jacques Richmond, Wendy Page and Jim Marr had come up with a teen anthem called 'Because We Want To'. After just one sing-through, everyone knew it had to be Billie's first single. It was incredibly catchy, with the chorus eventually the chorus driving people mad: '*Why you gotta play that song so loud? Because we want to… Because we want to…* '

But at first hearing, Jim and Wendy's production and Billie's voice brought just a little bit of an edge to the sound and lifted it above the pop mainstream. As the engineers fine-tuned the track, everyone felt that with a bit of luck and a good press they might even have created a classic.

After working on a couple of 'Because We Want To' remixes, Billie recorded '*G.H.E.T.T.O.U.T.*', which would be the B-side for the single, and then 'Project Piper' moved up a gear. It was time for Billie to shoot her first video and the girl who wanted to be an actress was going to have the time of her life.

On 28 June 1998, the residents of a quiet street in

Greenwich, south-east London, were asked to stay indoors all day. First thing that morning, a crew of more than 100 people had descended on the area, alongside a fleet of vans and trailers, a vast amount of camera equipment and a 50-foot crane. Big money was being spent and Innocent wanted to make sure Billie began her career with a bang. The premise for the video was that Billie would be beamed down from a spaceship in order to show off her special powers. She sang and danced down the street at the head of a troupe of dancers – having the time of her life. The filming lasted two days, with everyone rehearsing and dancing to the same few bars of music over and over again. And Billie says she loved every minute. She was easily the youngest person on the set but she says she seemed to have no problem getting on with the other dancers or the production staff. Considering that the final video would last less than five minutes, the days on set were long and even then no one had much of an idea what the end result would be. Nearly a month of post-production work by the computer animation experts who had previously worked on *Jurassic Park* and *Lost in Space* was required to add the extra effects Innocent had planned.

With the single and the video in the bag, Innocent finally had its first product ready to go. Now it needed to start selling it.

For Billie, this meant stepping into another almost entirely adult world. She was going to be put in front of every and any journalist who wanted to speak to her –

and a fair few who clearly didn't. She was expected to be charming and personable first thing in the morning and last thing at night. She would have to perform her new song relentlessly. And she certainly wasn't expected to complain. 'When you are launching a new act, you need to make sure that the whole plot, as the record industry calls it, is water-tight,' says Jeff Smith, then head of music policy at Radio One. 'This means getting as much television exposure as possible and getting in the right magazines such as *Smash Hits!* and *Top of the Pops*. Nowadays, it also means getting in the tabloids as well because they now take such a big interest in pop. This all lets the record company show the younger audience what the new artist looks like, tells them who they are and gives them a bit of a story to latch on to.'

Billie's story, of course, was based around how young and how confident she was. The hope was that she would be an inspiration to the rediscovered and increasingly girl-powered 9–14 market. To this end, she was supposed to pitch herself as the cool best friend they had always dreamed of having; someone fabulously successful, but not someone who has forgotten her roots. It was a message Billie found she could give out in her sleep. 'It's not girl power, it's youth power,' she said of 'Because We Want To', deliberately trying to make her fans feel older than they were. And she certainly didn't want them to think she had given herself ideas above her station. 'I have wanted to be famous for as long as I can remember. But up until now, the only singing I have done has been in the bath,' she told all the magazine interviewers. She was keen to prove she was ordinary in every other way as well. 'My family is really pleased for me and really supportive. I don't have pushy parents and they certainly didn't push me into all of this. In fact, they are the ones who keep me in touch with reality. They are always anxious about whether I am doing the right things or if I am determined enough, but most of all they want to be sure that I'm happy. I want to be a success but they don't want me to be devastated if this doesn't turn out too well.' It was the perfect mix of on-message ambition and honest humbleness. Reading the press coverage every day, Hugh Goldsmith applauded his protégé at almost every turn.

As part of the three-month promotional slog for the single, Billie then headed off around the country. She did a massive tour of the country's primary schools, sometimes appearing, singing and speaking at three different locations a day. Then there were the under-18s nightclubs and discos, where once more up to three half-hour appearances might be required every night.

Next up came some even longer days all across Europe. She flew to Scandinavia, France and Italy to ensure she had a high enough profile over there in time for her continental launch later in the summer. And all the time she was forced to think on her feet as the magazine and newspaper reporters queued up for comments, photographs and interviews. Answering all the usual questions about her school life, her star sign, her favourite colour and the job she would do if she weren't famous were easy — her answers were 'it was great', 'Virgo', 'lilac' and 'a hairdresser' — but she always needed to be ready for the wildcards, such as, 'If you were a chocolate bar, which one would it be?' Billie wanted to be a Twix because 'two pieces mean I can be in two places at one time,' which was about as good an answer as it gets.

Back at Innocent's head office in London, she had to help choose and sign off the cover image for 'Because We Want To', picking a hands on hips, midriff-revealing shot of her gazing out through a mass of artfully messy and cleverly streaked hair. It was a cover shot that made her look businesslike, tough and professional — as well as a whole lot less tired than she was starting to feel in real life.

'If I succeed, I won't be an overnight success. I will have worked my arse off,' the 15-year-old said brutally as the promotional campaign got back on the road once more. Behind the scenes, Innocent's final challenge was to decide exactly when to release Billie's first single and see whether all this effort had been worthwhile. It was a World Cup summer and official and unofficial football songs were dominating the charts. In some ways, this gave Billie an opportunity, and the following summer 'Because We Want To' was chosen as the official anthem of the Women's Football World Cup which gave her international career an unexpected boost. But back in 1998, the real attention was clearly focused on David

Beckham, Michael Owen and all the other men in France. And the longer England stayed in the competition, the longer the likes of David Baddiel and Frank Skinner's 'Three Lions' was likely to stay in the Number One slot and take attention from Billie.

So it was with one eye on the action in France that she prepared for one final secret gig that summer. It was a private London showcase for music and media industry VIPs, probably the last launch event before her single would go on sale. As well as 'Because We Want To', Billie performed a storming set of other up-tempo new songs and soulful R&B-style covers. The audience loved her – and it was an audience that mattered, a group of people who would look beyond the headlines and judge performers against the quality of their work. 'From our point of view, if the marketing isn't accompanied by a good record, we aren't going to play it. That's what sorts out the real pop hits from the also-rans,' says Radio One's Jeff Smith. He put Billie on the play list from the word go.

When David Beckham was sent off against Argentina and England crashed out of the World Cup on penalties, Innocent was ready to push the button. The single was shipped out to the stores and Billie got back to business. In the first week of release, she was working like never before. *Blue Peter*, *Fully Booked* and *MTV* were just three of the staggering 34 television shows she appeared on in the most important seven days of her life. Andrew Miller, presenter of the Channel Four show *Boom!*, was one of the presenters to meet her, and he says he was staggered by her performance and her professionalism. 'We were the last show she was doing on that particular day and it was obvious that she was exhausted and had been worked incredibly hard. She was also tiny, which seemed to make her seem even more vulnerable. But she couldn't have done more to sell herself to us when we spoke. She was charming, kind and utterly focused when the cameras were running. *Boom!* was a magazine show where a lot of our guests were teenagers and a lot were adult music and television stars. If I had to say which category Billie came closest to, I would certainly pick the latter. It was obvious she was determined to succeed and everyone on the crew warmed to her. There was a real sense among us that we wanted her to do well.'

But as the record company waited for any early sales reports from the shops, everyone knew Billie had mountains still to climb. Her biggest problem was that she wasn't the only big new act aiming for a hit that week. The *Emmerdale* to *Coronation Street* actor Matthew Marsden was also releasing a single – 'The Heart's Lone Desire' – and it was hard to find people prepared to bet against him reaching Number One. Matthew had only just left his role as the *Street*'s sexy mechanic Chris Collins and had just been named Top Newcomer at the National Television Awards. His female fan club were exactly the kind of people Billie was trying to win over for her single. And no one was sure which way they would jump. Throw new releases into the mix from the likes of Celine Dion and the Bee Gees, Destiny's Child, Ricky Martin and Mary J Blige, and it was easy to see why Billie and Innocent were worried. The first post-football chart of the summer was going to be a tough one to crack.

But when Sunday came, an exhausted Billie had indeed cracked it. 'Because We Want To' had beaten all-comers to the Number One slot, and it had done so in style. Figures from Chart Information Network revealed that, earlier in 1998, some artists had got to Number One by selling as few as 40,000 singles – All Saints, for example, had stayed at Number One by selling just 54,000 singles in the final week of January with 'Never Ever'. In July, Billie had sold more than 80,000 singles in her first week – in the process, she even made it on to the *News at Ten*.

Billie had also made a little bit of history. Researchers said that at 15 years and 287 days old she was the youngest female solo artist to top the charts since Helen Shapiro in 1961 with 'Walking Back to Happiness'. And Helen had taken several weeks to reach the top spot. Billie was the youngest female ever to enter the chart at Number One.

Wild celebrations were out, however. Billie was in Swindon when she did the obligatory telephone interview with Mark Goodier on Radio One and then screeched with joy, hugged her family, slumped back on the sofa and closed her eyes. She might be the youngest person to have hit a first-time Number One slot, but she was old enough to know that it meant her life would change for ever. She also knew that the hard work she had done in the past three months was far from over. So she turned down the offer of a glass of champagne because she wanted a cup of tea. She was in bed by 9.00pm and asleep half-an-hour later.

'I sort of freaked out. I didn't even move for a little while, I just tried to sit there and take it in. But I couldn't. So I got up and started screaming.'

When she did her next round of newspaper and magazine interviews the following week, that was how she described the moment she heard the news about the chart. But years later, a more self-aware Billie would admit that the screaming had been pretty much all fake. In a comment which would fascinate psychologists, she said that she had only been doing what she felt she ought to have been doing. 'In reality, I remember sitting there thinking, "I can't feel this in my guts," and that did bother me. I can only revel in things with hindsight. I am sure people who are more at peace with themselves can enjoy the moment. I couldn't and maybe still can't. At the time, you don't really realise how good things are. It was a shame but there was no time to really sit back and enjoy it, to think, "Hey, I'm Number One." Anyway, I didn't want to celebrate. I was too tired.'

A car came to pick Billie up just after dawn the following day. She had a series of live breakfast television interviews to give, another nerve-wracking first for the 15-year-old. Within days, as she travelled around the country performing the song to try and stay at Number One for a second week, she had another lesson to learn – that not everyone will support you when you hit the top.

What she also found was that there was rarely any logic to the subsequent criticism. In her first week of success, she was being attacked from two quite different points of view. On one side, critics started to deride her song as 'an anthem to tweenies desperate to stay up late and overdose on sugar'. Another made fun of her supposedly edgy image. 'If Billie Piper is street-wise, then you can bet the kind of street she is wise to is wide, tree-lined and thoroughly respectable,' one critic joked.

On the other side of the argument, however, commentators started to blame Billie for encouraging what they saw as the end of civilised life as we know it. The clearest example of the latter approach came when a paper decided to compare Billie's life and career with that of her successful predecessor Helen Shapiro. 'A glance at the differing backgrounds and behaviour of these two teenage starlets tells you a lot about how Britain has changed – little of it, people will think, for the better,' it began. The article went on to provide a list of these negative trends, ignoring the fact that Shapiro's hit had topped the charts 21 years before Billie had even been born. The idea that she could be somehow blamed for the changes in society since then was ludicrous. But that was just what the paper tried to do. In just one piece of evidence, it pointed to the fact that 'Billie has already been photographed out on the town in a revealing slip dress and clutching a glass of champagne'.

'Yes, I was upset about that,' Billie said when she was asked about the criticism – which had subsequently been picked up and repeated by several radio stations. 'For a start, I was actually wearing a dress. There's a bit of a difference between a slip and a dress. And it wasn't revealing at all, it was just a normal dress and, in fact, it came down to below my knee. I had about two glasses of champagne because I was celebrating my Number One record. Is that wrong?'

Billie was also keen to defend her hit song itself from the same critics, who again said the lyrics summed up everything that was wrong with modern Britain. 'Yes, "Because We Want To" is about being rebellious, but in a positive way,' she said. 'I hope it inspires other young people to do what they want and make their own dreams come true. And already a lot of people have sent me emails and notes saying, "You have inspired us to start a band," and stuff like that. And I feel really proud that I might have given people the will-power to do things they might otherwise have been too scared to try.' The 5-foot-5 *Smash Hits!* girl from Swindon had already come a long way. And she was ready to prove she wasn't going to be a pushover on the rest of her journey.

Fortunately, Billie was still winning plenty of influential fans in the industry. 'At the moment, there aren't that many solo female pop stars with the right sort of attitude that our readers can really identify with,' said

Smash Hits! associate editor Alex Needham. 'Billie is really charismatic, she's a little bit rebellious and she is on readers' side. She has got a long career ahead of her and she seems pretty special.' The magazine would support her for some time to come.

The public were also on her side – at least for a while. When she headed back to Swindon for the coming week to sign singles at the local Virgin Megastore, there were queues backing up right through the town's Brunel Centre. 'Everyone has been great, I've had loads of support and I wanted to pay Swindon back,' she shouted at the crowds when she was finally dragged away by minders and rushed back to London to rehearse for her most important television break yet – it was nearly time for *Top of the Pops*.

The previous week, Zoe Ball had introduced Billie's space-craft, street-dancing video. This week, Jamie Theakston was the host and Billie was appearing live in the studio. She headed over to West London where the show was recorded feeling uncharacteristically nervous. 'It is the show you watch all your life, the one you know all your friends and family will be watching, let alone all the fans. You don't want to mess it up,' she said of the experience. But after looking out at the small but enthusiastic crowd in the studio, she found her old confidence. However many butterflies were churning up her insides, she knew everything would be OK as soon as she started to perform. The girl who had never really wanted to be a singer in the first place was passionate about the play-acting part of her job. She realised that being on stage was her cue to give the performance of her life. It was live theatre, the thing she had got the taste for at her Swindon drama classes and at the Sylvia Young school. And so it was the one thing which would re-energise her when the promotional treadmill for her single got too exhausting. 'There's nothing like being on stage in front of a live audience. Nothing like the response and the buzz and it takes all your worries away. I love it,' she said of her early days in the singing spotlight.

Her other big buzz came from travel and, like all her fellow pop stars of the day, Billie was having plenty of opportunities to enjoy it. In the months after 'Because We Want To' topped the charts, an industry survey reported on the relentless schedules that many of the big pop acts were facing. In just over a month that summer, Steps flew to Australia, Hong Kong and Thailand, for example, clocking up an average of 36 hours a week on planes. All Saints were doing almost as much travelling in Europe, spending almost 20 hours a week in the air. And with Innocent launching Billie around the world, she was soon to spend more time out of the country than she did in it. As well as regular hops over to Europe, Billie's first six months as a singer would include long-haul trips to America, New Zealand and Australia, where she was struck by a heavy bout of 'flu that took many months fully to shake off.

What the travel survey didn't mention was the fact that the singers in Steps and All Saints were all several years older than Billie – and they also had each other as company when they were on tour. Despite the best efforts of her record company, Billie, as a solo artist, had no one of her own age to hang around with. With her dad running his company and her mum looking after her younger brother and sisters back in Swindon, Billie also missed out on having any family to chat to on the road. David Price, the 17-year-old Swindon boy she had started seeing just before signing her record deal, wasn't able to join her either and so their relationship also fizzled out before really going anywhere. Billie, at 15, was very much on her own.

The one constant she did have in her life back then was Dublin-born Deborah Lynam, who had gone from being a junior production manager at Innocent to Billie's near full-time chaperone, personal assistant and friend. Their partnership had begun just after Billie had signed to Innocent and was about to head off on her first under-18 club tour. 'Obviously, the record company realised she needed someone to go with her and that someone ended up being me,' says Deborah. And while she was almost twice Billie's age, the pair found they had plenty in common. Deborah watched from the wings as her charge went from being a complete unknown forced to wait in corridors to meet people who could hardly spare her the time of day, to being the biggest star of the day who practically had a red carpet rolled out for her wherever she went. Behind the scenes, she and Billie would marvel at how much had changed since they had met. Deborah developed a sort of unspoken understanding of the way Billie was feeling on any given day. 'I can see when things are getting too much for her. Sometimes, people forget how young she is and expect too much from her. The pace is gruelling when we travel. You touch down, go straight to the hotel then straight out to an official dinner with a local record or television company. It's tough, however old you are, and that's even before you take jet-lag into account.'

In their hotel rooms, Billie would try and catch up on her sleep while Deborah unpacked the essential items she knew made the travelling bearable for them both – Tetley tea bags, baked beans and Cadbury's chocolate for Billie, and an aromatherapy kit for herself.

Back in Britain, Billie was working on her first album and preparing to launch her next single. Everyone knew that the stakes were still high and that if she proved to be a one-hit-wonder then the album would probably never see the light of day. The curse of 'second single syndrome' – a huge flop that unaccountably followed a massive hit – was everyone's worst nightmare, and Billie knew full well that it was a very real possibility. She thought the next single, 'Girlfriend', was a great song. It had the same feisty, female-friendly and up-front tone – the strong woman pushing for the date she wanted – and it had another great chorus. But would the fans agree?

It turned out that they did. Billie had put celebrations for her 16th birthday on hold in order to do another whistle-stop tour of the television studios and nightclubs (the primary schools weren't on the agenda this time, to everyone's relief). She had been interviewed and photographed relentlessly by everyone from her local paper in Swindon to the *Sunday Times*. And on 11 October, she got the news that everyone had been hoping for. 'Girlfriend' hit the charts at Number One and even more history was being made. Overnight, Billie had become the first female solo artist to have two Number Ones in the same year since Cilla Black in 1964. And there were still more than two months to go before Billie would give up hope of achieving the triple.

Even better news came through when the Chart Information Network figures were published. 'Girlfriend' had sold a staggering 120,000 copies in its first week – half as many again as 'Because We Want To' and a clear sign that Billie was getting more rather than less popular. Billie herself was jubilant and once more revealed a flash of steel in her response to the news. 'Not everyone had faith in me. People imagined a little brat with a flash-in-the-pan single. I've proved them wrong,' she said in response to the doubters. The tough cookie that Hugh Goldsmith had been grooming for the past six months was still very much in evidence when the need arose.

This second success confirmed Billie's new position in the entertainment A-list, and she found herself in very good company. With 'Girlfriend' on top of the charts, she followed no less than Dolly Parton as the chief guest on the National Lottery show, chatting along with co-host Boy George before pressing the vital button and selecting the lucky numbers. Going on the lottery show coincided with a wave of speculation about how much money Billie must be earning. The papers loved the fact that one of the very first things she had bought herself after signing her record deal was a new wallet. They ignored her protestations that it was just because her old purse had finally given up the ghost and fallen apart and focused on the huge wads of cash they thought she might be putting in the new acquisition.

After 'Girlfriend' went gold, one magazine put her in a new Rich List alongside the Spice Girls and half the Premiership footballers and claimed that secret deals and advertising revenues meant she was already well on her way to earning back the £1 million it said Innocent had spent launching her as a pop star.

The idea that Billie was the richest 16-year-old in Britain was soon dismissed by music insiders, however. She wouldn't even come close to millionaire status until her album was released, they pointed out. And as she wasn't expected to write many of the songs on it herself, then even this would have to sell extraordinarily well to push her into the financial élite.

Behind the scenes, the one thing which might have given Billie's bank balance a boost was the fact that she had precious little time for shopping – and when she did feel like a splurge, she had no idea what to buy. 'It's weird but because I am so young there is nothing to spend my money on. I can't buy a car, or a house, or tons of champagne.' She also found the things she did want to buy were now being handed to her for free – which amazingly enough wasn't how she liked it. 'Already, there are times when I don't enjoy being able to get everything I want. I don't have to save up my money for clothes, for instance, because they are always given to me anyway. That takes the excitement out of it a bit,' she said.

When reporters asked her about what else she did in her spare time, the Billie Piper of 16 proved she was looking and planning ahead – just as she had done all her life. 'Right now, there are some things I am trying not to do, like go to clubs, so that I'll have something left to experience when I get older. I don't want to be bored of going out by the time I'm 18,' she said with surprising maturity. 'I think going out to showbiz parties all the time and getting drunk is a bit naff.' It was a final throwaway line that would one day come back to haunt her – and it was one of the many things Billie said which would occasionally remind everyone of just how young this new pop princess still was.

Those who met Billie said this reminder came through in other ways as well. 'Billie was determined to get the message across that she wasn't a child,' says pop reporter Alison Sunderland of the interview she did with the star just after her 16th birthday. 'She was very big on how other 15- and 16-year-olds seem immature to her and how easily she thinks she fits into her new adult world. She was also determined to make me understand that she knew about all the pitfalls of the industry, about how much she didn't mind being on her own, how hard it was, and how tough you need to be to survive it. But the more she repeated how much the industry has made her grow up in the past six months the more I started to wonder how much of it was just bravado. I left our interview feeling just a little bit sorry for her – and even a little bit worried for her.'

In some respects, Alison was right to worry. In another conversation, Billie admitted that some of the other reporters she dealt with were starting to push her out of her depth. 'Journalists can be patronising and manipulative, basically because I am so young and they think it is all right to do that,' she said. 'They pressure me and they seem to want really personal things and I do get a bit scared sometimes. They want to know things about my private life that have nothing to do with my pop career – about boyfriends and stuff. I just think it is so irrelevant to what I want to talk about so it can be hard and get a bit scary.'

As is typical of the media, it wasn't just Billie who was facing this pressure. Her former schoolfriends from both London and Swindon were being asked for stories, anecdotes and even photographs of their newly famous friend. David Price, her former boyfriend, was also at the centre of the storm as reporters demanded his thoughts about Billie. It was an intense learning curve about the nature of fame for everyone involved – and with several former friends selling their stories to the papers, not everyone would emerge from it with their integrity intact.

Fortunately for Billie, she was quite literally able to fly

away from all the media interest for a couple of days. She was off to Florida to film the video for 'Honey to the Bee' – the differently-spelt title track from her soon-to-be released album *Honey to the B*. While in the American sunshine, Billie was also doing some new publicity photos, trying out a more glamorous, adult look with new styling and a new-found cleavage to match.

After wheeling her own suitcase through Heathrow, Billie was immediately back in business. *Honey to the B* was finally on its way to the music reviewers and the shops. Her next big test was set to begin.

What Billie was steeling herself for was the kind of knee-jerk criticism that often follows an early success. She had been built up with her first two singles. Was it time to be dragged down with her album? The serious record reviewers rarely gave much time to what they saw as overly commercial, bubblegum pop. Billie had been damned as a manufactured act, a squeaky clean puppet with no free will or free expression of her own. It would have been very easy to knock her down accordingly – especially in what increasingly looked like a post-Spice world where credibility was suddenly back in vogue.

At first, some of the early reviews were crushingly negative. '*Honey to the B*ejesus, it's bad,' being just one line Billie tried to forget. But if you could ignore some of the cleverly barbed comments, some of the other big reviews of the album were good. More than good, in fact. The *Times* was a perfect example of the way praise was handed out. 'For those who have already had enough of Billie's soap-star cuteness and youthful effervescence, the news is grim — judging from this record, Billie is going to be around for quite some time,' wrote the paper's music critic Angus Batey. 'True, *Honey to the B* is pretty synthetic and very, very calculated, shamelessly stealing from a clutch of jaw-droppingly obvious sources such as All Saints and the Spice Girls, as well as some more credible ones such as Janet Jackson and Wilson Pickett. But it is a fine pop record, one that knows that the street-smart point where black music meets the white mainstream has always been Where It's At, and it is a far better debut than Piper's heroine, Madonna, managed to make.'

The *Daily Mirror's* take was shorter but no less positive. 'You will love it,' was the four word conclusion to its review.

Back in Swindon, Billie was euphoric. In many ways, she said the good reviews meant more to her than the success of her singles. It would be several years before she stopped caring what the critics said about her; at 16, their views mattered. She still read almost all her coverage and, while she tried to balance out the good and the bad, she couldn't always put the negatives out of her mind. Being treated like a professional meant a huge amount to her. Being told she had produced a professional album compensated for all the stress, the nerves and the sheer exhaustion of promoting it. Putting her acting on hold and following this new path suddenly seemed to have been worthwhile.

The fans agreed. *Honey to the B* certainly didn't top the charts (it peaked at just number 14). But it proved to be a steady seller, going platinum within a month of its release. And there were still several tracks on it that were crying out to be released as singles. As 1998 drew to a close, there still seemed everything to play for.

Billie's big challenge was to try and bag a third Number One in the same calendar year, putting her ahead of Cilla Black's record for a solo female artist. And everyone at Innocent decided that if you were going to shoot for something like this, you might as well do it in style. On top of everything else she had achieved, Billie was going to aim for a Christmas Number One. If she succeeded, she would be the youngest artist ever to do so. And with 'She Wants You', it looked as if she might just pull it off.

The song had been co-written by *Fame Academy* coach Pam Sheyne, who would soon provide another song, 'Genie in a Bottle', to Christina Aguilera. The song Pam had produced for Billie was one of the most upbeat on her album and was accompanied by a bright, live video that looked as if it had been filmed in a seaside holiday resort (in fact, it had been made on a wet and windy day in Greenwich, south-east London, and the sunlight on screen was all artificial). Innocent had even decided to put Billie's version of Wham!'s 'Last Christmas' on the single as well to give it more of a seasonal flavour.

The single, with its glamorous cover image, hit the shops on 7 December and one of the first people to buy a copy was Billie's dad, Paul. Free copies of all her work were stacked up at the record company offices and at home. But ever since 'Because We Want To' had been released, he had decided to go to a local shop and buy his own copies as an act of faith in his daughter.

As it turned out, 'She Wants You' didn't give Billie her hat-trick of Number Ones, or the Christmas Number One, which went to the Spice Girls with 'Goodbye'. But ending the year at Number Three was hardly anything to be ashamed of, not least because in a few months time the single would also give her an early break in America, making the Top Ten of the *Billboard* dance chart.

Ten months earlier, Billie had been just another 15-year-old at stage school. Now with three hit singles and a top-selling album under her belt, she was a force to be reckoned with. And she was only getting started.

4
BEATING BRITNEY

THERE WAS A new kid on the block in early 1999 who was going to make life a whole lot tougher for Billie; her name was Britney Spears. In a whole lot of ways, the girls were incredibly similar. Britney, just like Billie, had left home as a teenager to go to a performing arts school in the big city – in her case New York. Britney, just like Billie, had signed a record deal at 15. And Britney, just like Billie, would see her first single go straight in at Number One.

The one big difference was that Britney did all this on a global scale and, in the process, she turned up the heat on every other young singer around the world. Britain had its first taste of the Britney magic in February 1999 when 'Baby One More Time' was released and went straight to the top of the charts, ultimately becoming the best-selling single of the year. The video, which turned schoolgirl chic into something far more disturbing, made Billie's effort on 'Because We Want To' look distinctly amateur. And with several more hit songs waiting to be released, Britney was suddenly looking like the one to beat.

At first, Billie looked as if she had been wrong-footed by her sexy American cousin. Her big project was a soft-focus ITV television show called *Thank Abba for the Music*, in which she sang cover versions alongside the likes of fellow teen-stars Steps, Cleopatra and B★Witched. The programme did pretty well in the Saturday night ratings but it was hardly at the cutting edge of cool.

Repeating some of the same sets at the year's Brit Awards would awaken other demons for Billie. She was wearing a red spandex, Seventies-style, all-in-one outfit for her part of the show and thought it looked hilarious when she did a twirl backstage in front of the costume and make-up people. But when Billie watched a recording of the show the following evening, she got a huge shock. They say the camera adds ten pounds – but Billie thought it had added far more to her while adding nothing to the stick-thin figures of the B★Witched girls and the dancers she had shared the stage with. The sight of her simply made a bad night seem even worse. Billie had been nominated for two Brits but had lost them both (Des'ree had beaten her to the Best British Female Award and Belle & Sebastian were named Best British Newcomer). Alone in her London hotel room, Billie suddenly started to cry. She was exhausted, isolated, run-down – and now she thought she was fat.

A pep talk on the phone from her mother – who had offered to head straight down the M4 to pick her up and take her home – got Billie through the night. And first thing the following morning, she had to put all her new insecurities behind her again. It was back to business with a new single and, hopefully, a new look.

Desperate to see off the challenge from Britney, Billie and the Innocent bosses had picked what they all thought was the most mature track on her album for the 22 March launch. That track was 'Honey to the Bee' and, when everyone had sat around the board room table discussing the launch campaign, Billie had come up with what she thought was the perfect media message. 'Britney is stuck in the school room. I'm now singing with the grown-ups,' was the story she wanted to tell.

With this in mind, she steeled herself to make the move from children's television to the adult market, taking on the older and quicker wits on *Never Mind the Buzzcocks* the week before 'Honey to the Bee' was launched. Meatloaf, comic Rowland Rivron and Nick Keynes from Ultra were the other guests that week and rumours were rife that host Mark Lamarr had been coming on to her throughout the evening. Billie, though, saw it differently. 'Doing the show was such an experience because it was filled with really cocky men. I think Mark was just having a laugh because he didn't show any interest after we stopped filming. We both come from Swindon so we were talking about that a lot afterwards. Then one of the women who works for me said to him, "Look, pack it in, I'm her mother." And he went completely white and freaked out, bless him. He's cool but he's not my type. Quiffs are the sort of thing my dad would have on his head.'

Billie struck a host of more sophisticated poses in all the other television appearances and magazine photo shoots she did as part of the promotion – and, at first, the critics seemed to buy into it. 'Back to your desk, Britney, playground pop has come of age,' said one early reviewer when 'Honey to the Bee' hit the shops. The fans, though, weren't quite as convinced. The single gave Billie her fourth consecutive Top Three hit, but it never made it to Number One. So had Billie lost her touch?

Music experts said she had little reason to worry. 'Having two number-one singles from a first album puts Billie in a very exclusive club, especially for a solo female artist. By the time you release the fourth single from the album, the laws of diminishing returns normally come into play and anything inside the Top Ten should still be seen as a good result,' says chart historian Colin Young. 'The test for someone like Billie was not how these end-of-line singles performed, but how well the work was going on her next album. The first single from that would be the real mark of her staying power as an artist.'

In the meantime, a seemingly endless series of other commitments were helping to turn Billie into a fully-fledged member of the celebrity aristocracy. She had been carried around a television studio by Mr Blobby, had heard her songs played in the background of the Queen Vic in *EastEnders* and the hair salon on *Coronation Street*. One company had even produced a hardback *Billie: Princess of Pop* annual promising 'everything you ever wanted to know about Britain's brightest young star'.

Away from the limelight, there were plenty of other things to focus on as 1999 got under way – not least Billie's first serious boyfriend. He was Ritchie Neville, one of the singers in the boy band 5ive and he and Billie had met several times the previous year on the kids and pop television circuit. He had admired her toughness at coping with her workload alone. She had liked the relaxed way he interacted with his fellow band-members and coped with the pressures of fame. He was nearly three years older than Billie and had been in the music world for a lot longer – 5ive had been formed in 1996 after the father and son pop entrepreneurs Bob and Chris Herbert put an advert in the *Stage* for singers and dancers. The idea had worked for the Spice Girls and, after their success with Bros, the Herberts were ready to give a boy band a go as well.

The good-looking Ritchie had been an obvious choice for the new band and, by the time he met Billie, he and his fellow singers were on their way to notching up 13 hit singles, four hit albums and some 1.5 million total record sales. When they finally got serious, he and Billie would be one of the biggest power couples in the business –

though when news of their relationship finally leaked out, it would trigger enormous problems for them both.

What Ritchie also offered Billie was a shoulder to cry on. The time-lag nature of the music business meant that she was still travelling a lot as other countries played catch-up and saw the release of songs which had been and gone in the UK. And back in Britain, everyone wanted her back in the studio as soon as possible to start working on her second album.

Britney's second single, 'Sometimes', had just fallen short of the Number One slot, so Billie had retained her crown as the youngest double chart-topper. Innocent wanted to capitalise on this and reinforce her position in the face of a set of ferocious new threats. In 1999, a new American invasion was hitting the UK market, backed by huge promotional budgets. So Billie was about to go up against the likes of Jennifer Lopez, Destiny's Child and the tough new teen queen Christina Aguilera. Britain wasn't slow to find rivals for Billie's pop crown either — each of the individual Spice Girls seemed to be releasing singles, including the former Spice Geri Halliwell. S Club 7 was cleaning up in the kids' market and boy bands, including 5ive, were reasserting their dominance among Billie's pre-teen fans.

If Billie was to make enough money for her promoters, they wanted to keep her working. But at 16, and after the most exhausting year of her life, she was desperately in need of a break. Her former classmates from Sylvia Young were getting ready for their GCSEs and were going to all the theatre and television auditions she had dreamed of tackling. Billie was simply being told to get on a plane, get in a car, appear on a television show and mime to yet another song someone else had written for her. She was a hit, and she knew she had absolutely no right to complain about the way her life had turned out. But sometimes she wondered if she had done the right thing. And this was before she started to see the dark side of fame.

The first storm clouds gathered in the middle of the summer. Billie and Ritchie had been dating, in secret, for several months and Billie was convinced she had found her soulmate. Both were starting to get weary of the fame treadmill and they said they could talk for hours about music, the industry, the fans, the workload and all the executives and suits that sometimes seemed to surround them 24 hours a day. They also talked about their backgrounds, their childhoods and their ambitions for the future. They connected. And while Billie hadn't wanted to go public about their relationship, she found that once she started talking about it, she couldn't stop. In spite of herself, she had turned into one of the gushing, loved-up girls she normally tried to avoid.

'It is so cool being with Ritch, even though I hardly ever see him,' she told *Sunday Mirror* reporter Ian Hyland after he first broke the story of the relationship. 'It is difficult fitting time in between his schedule and my own diary, but we talk all the time and when we do meet up we make the most of it.'

When Billie was in Swindon, for example, Ritchie would drive over to her parents' house to spend time with her and her family. He would take her younger brother Charlie out for a drive in his sports car, which made him a friend for life. Other than that, the pair just relaxed and enjoyed life together. 'We go to the pictures, or to dinner. It's just normal stuff and it's all good news for a change,' Billie said.

But that didn't mean that there wasn't bad news on the horizon as well, and for Billie, this manifested itself in the simple fact that boy-band fans rarely take kindly to the girlfriends of their idols. The backlash against her, when it came, blew right into the sanctuary of her home town.

It began with a few catcalls and a bit of jeering in the street. But, after a while, things got more serious and even visiting the shops in Swindon became a nightmare. Some girls deliberately barged into her as they walked by while others yelled increasingly unpleasant abuse from passing cars. It was a huge shock to the system and meant Billie had to change the way she lived and behaved. 'I have to keep my head down now, especially when I'm at home,' she admitted – a terrible thing to have to say at just 16 years old. 'I get a lot of mouthing off and it is getting hard for me to go out. It is mostly women who can be very bitchy. There are a lot of girls who elbow me when I walk past them. The way they see it, I stole their heart-throb away from them and I am finding out just how much they love him.'

Having learned the hard way that she had to be wary

over the way girls her own age would react to her, Billie then got an even tougher wake-up call from a boy. 'He came over, said I was ugly and hit me. I was so upset. It was in my home town and I still thought everyone would be pleased to see me there,' she said, shocked not so much by the actual physical violence as by the anger or the hatred that must have triggered it. What made it worse was the fact that it was hard to protect yourself against irrational jealousies. It was impossible to identify who might be feeling them and, as she tried to deal with the threats, Billie proved there was a very real vulnerability behind her pop star's mask. All the glamorous photographs in the world couldn't always hide how young she sometimes felt in these difficult times. 'You can learn a dance routine in a day but you can't learn to be emotionally strong in a day. It's something that needs plenty of experience,' she said quietly after a group of passers by had once more shouted at her in the street. 'Emotionally, I am still just a teenager. I still cry. Getting to where I have got has been lonely at times,' she said, her voice trailing off.

And this loneliness was something which would characterise much of Billie's life. It might appear that she was always surrounded by people – Deborah Lynam was still around as a supporter and assistant – but however strong their friendship had become it was impossible to ignore the fact that she was also being paid to be with her young charge. It was the same with the hair and make-up people Billie shared a laugh with on photoshoots, and the dancers she tried to hang out with when they went out on the road. She was 16 years old and she was effectively everyone's boss. A line was always being drawn around her, marking her out as slightly different to everyone else, making it harder to find friends.

That summer, Billie desperately needed friends because she was about to get another rude reminder of the price of fame – this time delivered by first-class post. Hate mail started to pour in to the previously happy fan club her parents were running for her from their Swindon home, and much of it was deeply unpleasant. The first wave of poison pen letters called Billie a bitch, a cow, a slapper, a tart – and worse. The next wave included some ferocious threats. 'There were a whole series of really horrible letters from people saying that they wanted to kill me. Some of them were addressed directly to my mum and dad while others went to Ritchie's mum, so it was really distressing for them as well. It's a chilling feeling when you open an envelope and you read something like that. It scared me a lot and still sends shivers down my spine. That's why I am always careful now and always look over my shoulder when I am out.'

For a 16-year-old success story, life at the top was suddenly starting to look a little less glittering for Billie. And what she didn't know was that things would shortly get even worse.

The public mockery began lightly. Sara Cox and some of the other Radio One DJ's began to call her Billie

Pipsqueak (Billie said it made her laugh) and there was a ridiculous rumour that she was, in fact, 26 years old and that she had only been pretending to be a teenager to get into the record books. People started to make savage comments about her looks, the shape of her face and the quality of her skin. Then there was the rush of sleazy adult websites which superimposed her face on some very X-rated bodies.

What should have been her moments of triumph then turned into nights she was desperate to forget. The 1999 *Smash Hits!* Poll Winners Party was one such example. In theory, it should have been a prefect homecoming evening for the girl whose career had been born in a *Smash Hits!* advert. And being nominated for several awards – from Most Fanciable Female to Best Female Solo Artist and Princess of Pop – meant she should have been thrilled at the chance to attend. But suddenly Billie was feeling exhausted and run-down. She seemed to be getting colds that never went away, niggling viruses which left her pale and drained, and the insomnia she had suffered on and off since childhood was back with a vengeance. The more she worried about the pressure she was under, the less she seemed able to relax. And then the more she worried. Deep down, Billie was well aware she was in the middle of a vicious circle. But she had no idea how to break free from it.

The *Smash Hits!* Poll Winners Party would end up making matters worse. Billie won two big awards, Pop Princess and the far more prestigious Best Female Solo

Artist award. But as she stood up and made her way to the stage, she got the shock of her life. The people on her table were clapping and cheering, but all around everyone else in the hall seemed to be jeering. A group of loud and angry 5ive fans were determined to make a very public statement about the girl who had stolen the heart of their favourite band-member.

A new wave of relentless booing had begun by the time Billie climbed on to the podium to collect her award. And by now she was so far from her own table of supporters that she could no longer hear their cheers. Many people who collect awards cry when they make their acceptance speeches, but they are almost always tears of happiness. Billie's tears, when they came, were born out of fear, hurt and sadness. She was stunned, chilled, mortified by the crowd's reaction. And the rest of what should have been one of the most wonderful nights of her career passed in a blur.

'I just couldn't understand why people were being that horrible. It's not like we in any way flaunted our relationship. It was nothing to do with anybody else,' Billie said the next day, when reporters demanded to know how she was feeling. She pointed to the tiny number of times she and Ritchie had ever been photographed together and the lengths they went to trying to keep their personal lives private.

Billie, who was living out of hotel rooms while she tried to find her first property, was hardly seen out for the next two weeks. 'One day I would be fine and the next

I would sink low again. I am naturally a worrier and everything that was going on affected my sleep pattern even more,' she admitted plaintively. 'I rang my mum a lot for long chats and I cried a lot as well. All I wanted was for people to love me.'

But in the outside world, the newspapers, in particular, were not prepared to extend her this courtesy. With no sightings of Billie, and no evidence of what she was doing, the rumour mills went into overdrive. Some people hinted that she had collapsed due to drugs; others said she was addicted to them. Some said she was pregnant with Ritchie's child and wanted to have the baby totally out of the public eye. Others agreed that she was pregnant but claimed she was planning an abortion. Regardless of the exact details of the stories, the basic theme was the same. Somehow, somewhere, the decision seemed to have been made that Billie would have to take on a new role in the celebrity soap opera. She was no longer the teenage queen everyone loved and wanted to emulate. She would, instead, have to be the burned-out child star, the Michael Jackson, Lena Zavaroni or Macaulay Culkin of her day. The sense that people actually wanted her career to implode in public was almost palpable, and the pressure on the Piper and Neville families was extraordinary.

To everyone's credit, including that of the bosses at Innocent, Billie herself was left in peace to ride out the storms. Her parents made huge efforts to ensure that for once she didn't read any of the more outlandish reports about her in the papers. They also encouraged her finally to see some doctors to check that there was no hidden illness eating away at their daughter. Fortunately, there wasn't. She was suffering from a form of water retention, possibly triggered by a kidney infection. But the main issue, they said, was exhaustion. What Billie needed most, they said, was enough time to rest and recharge her batteries. The events of the last year would have knocked the stuffing out of anyone. At 15 going on 16, it was always going to be too much to handle.

What the doctors didn't know, when they prescribed rest as the cure for Billie's ills, was that she had a pick-me-up of her own in mind to run alongside it. It was her pride. The longer she remained bed-ridden, the more she suddenly feared that the world was passing her by, and the more she suddenly worried that people would see her as a failure. That was the one thing she swore would never happen. So she picked up a pen and a pad of paper as she rested in her rented flat and waited for her strength to return. She started jotting things down, lines of poetry, ideas for plays or books and lyrics for songs.

'Don't worry about me. I'll be back… ' That was the two-sentence message she sent to the Innocent executives in the long summer of 1999. She had signed a three-album deal and the company had a huge amount invested in her. After all the hard work of the previous year, she wasn't going to let it all slip away.

Back on her feet, beating Britney became Billie's mini-obsession. In the early autumn, the American's third single had also failed to make it to Number One in Britain, yet the newspapers continued to say she was the greatest young artist in the world. Billie couldn't understand how her own achievements could be belittled so much in comparison. So as she pulled her life back on track, she gave herself another goal – another Number One single. She was back in business and she wanted the world to know.

'I worked it too hard… I was doing too much. Too much singing, too much travelling, too much not relaxing. I got sick and it knocked me out. Basically, I was knackered then. Now I'm not. It's simple.' Those were the stark, crystal-clear words Billie used when she gave her first comeback interview to the *Sunday Mirror*'s Ian Hyland in October 1999. She was at pains to prove just how much confidence her record company still had in her – taking him outside to show him the Ford car she had been bought for her 17th birthday, even though she had not yet had the time to learn to drive.

She talked frankly to Ian about her exhaustion and the stresses and strains that preyed on her mind. And, in the process, she proved that she had not lost her capacity to surprise or to charm. 'I went to meet Billie expecting a prima donna, a brat spoiled by all her success,' he said after the interview. 'But she was cool. Not cool like she was playing some sort of media game. Just cool, like, "Hiya, let's have a chat," which was a very pleasant surprise.'

Hyland joined the long list of reporters who said they were also surprised that Billie was confident enough to handle interviews on her own, without an entourage of minders and PR people checking up on her every word. Bearing in mind the media storm which had been swirling around her in recent months, he felt her confidence spoke volumes. 'She's young but she's no pushover and she's no record company puppet. She's a 17-year-old with a streak of steel,' he concluded.

Billie was also keen to get back to work, learn new skills and improve herself. Ritchie and the rest of the 5ive band members had told her how they tried to control more of their output after their first album. Each of them had subsequently started to write songs and work on the production side of the records. Billie decided to follow their lead, something she explained with characteristic honesty. 'I didn't write anything on the first album because obviously everything was a huge learning curve for me back then. I wanted to watch and find out more about the production side before I tried to do everything myself. Also, I didn't feel I had that much to write about at the time either. Now, after all I have gone through, I feel I have more to write about. Apart from everything else, I have done all this travelling around the world, meeting loads of different people, seeing different cultures and basically growing up.'

The writing she had been doing during her recovery phase had taken in all her feelings and fears about relationships, dating, bullying, partying and growing up. They also looked at darker subjects — isolation, loneliness, insecurity. Much of her work was raw and half-formed, but she had benefited hugely from getting her words down on paper. And she would carry on writing from that point onwards.

Hugh Goldsmith and the Innocent executives were overjoyed at the transformation in their young artist. Her enthusiasm was back; her ambition seemed stronger than ever. There were no longer any plans to release any new music in 1999, but everyone was feeling incredibly excited about the prospects for 2000.

In the autumn, Billie flew to Sweden to meet the new Later Inc writing team and talk about working together – she would ultimately record their track 'Ring My Bell' for the album. She then headed over to America to meet some other new musicians, writers and producers and work through some ideas for her vital second album. In the end, she felt so in tune with them that several of the tracks would be recorded in the States. The aim of the album was to have a cooler, R&B edge to it; pure pop anthems were out. The new songs weren't going to be message songs – they would deal with the same issues of love and relationships as her previous album – but they were now written for people who were in the middle of the dating game, not those still just dreaming about it.

'On my first album, I was basically just saying that I was young and happy and that everything was great. This time I want to sing about real things, whether they are good or bad. The songs are going to be more personal and have a real meaning and truth,' she said as the project reached the halfway stage.

Being back in the studio felt great, Billie said. With no cameras and no journalists to worry about, Billie could focus squarely on her job. And having had a bigger role in the writing of the tracks this time around, she was also keener to hang around as the post-production work was done. Making music, suddenly, was great fun. The problem was that once the music had been made it had to be sold. And this was the part of the job Billie was starting to dread.

Her big media blitz was pencilled in for May 2000, when the first single from her new album was due to be released. But just before then, Billie had signed up to do some slow-burn appearances to remind everyone who she was. She was booked to appear on *TFI Friday* with Chris Evans; it was an appearance that would end up changing her life.

Billie had been a fan of the Channel Four show for some time — and had a sneaking admiration for its host. The previous year, after appearing on *Never Mind the Buzzcocks*, she had been asked who she fancied the most — Chris Evans or the Buzzcocks' Mark Lamarr. Her answer would turn out to be very revealing. 'I'd go for Chris Evans,' she said without a second's hesitation. 'I can see why beautiful women find him attractive. There's something about him that's very charming, although it is so unnecessary when he walks out naked on *TFI Friday*. I really want to go on that show because I've heard from people who have been in the audience that he's actually got nothing to be proud of. I want to be able to check it out for myself.'

She was finally about to get the chance – and, funnily enough, the first time she actually met Chris he was naked, at least from the waist up. She had popped into his dressing room before the show, to find him bare-chested while the make-up people got him ready for the cameras. Embarrassingly enough, she says, she blushed. 'There was a definite mutual instant attraction,' she said. And the flirting would continue on the show itself. Chris was wearing one of his trademark flowery shirts, which Billie said she liked. So halfway through their interview, he took it off and demanded she swap it with hers.' It made for great television and Billie, Chris and the whole crew got to know each other even better after the show when they had a few drinks in the hospitality suite. It was there that Chris, not a man known for his emotional sensitivities, reckoned he spotted something slightly worrying behind his young guest's trademark smile.

'I liked her enormously, straight away, but there was no sense of romance,' Chris said afterwards. 'From then on, I kind of admired her from afar and felt sorry for her from afar as well. I could see her going through all sorts of problems and I'd think to myself, "She's not being looked after," which seemed a terrible shame.'

When *TFI Friday* was over, though, Billie was back to work with Innocent, her management and PR team. Everyone knew that when it came to re-launching her career, some very hard decisions had to be made. However unsavoury some of them found it, none of the executives or advisers could deny that the rules of the game had changed since Britney and Christina Aguilera had joined the pop circus. Wholesome, healthy and homely was out; sex seemed to be the only thing that sold. Billie had to decide if she was prepared to head in a similar direction.

She admitted the pressure for a change had been building up for some time. 'The things photographers say to try and persuade you things is hilarious,' she had said, mockingly, less than a year earlier. 'You will agree before you turn up that you are definitely not doing knickers and bras. Then once you are in make-up, you see the rails of clothes and it's like, bikini, see-through-top, panties, bras. Then it all starts... the "Billie, how about doing it this way?" stuff. But I am always like, "No, no, no," and I always get my way.'

Suddenly, the new Billie was ready to accept that she had to say, 'Yes, yes, yes,' instead. The new breed of British lads' mags were promising Billie a fantastic shop window from which to promote her new singles, album and image. But they would only offer it if she gave them the photos that they required. Ever the young businesswoman, Billie decided it was a deal worth doing. She agreed to interviews and photo sessions with two key magazines, *Maxim* and *Sky* — and afterwards it was hard to see which was the most embarrassing. When *Sky* hit the shelves in midsummer, 'Billie reveals her little secrets' was splashed over the cover shot of her sitting in a tiny white skirt with her underwear clearly showing. 'JUST SEVENTEEN' was the headline on the article itself, accompanied by even more revealing and suggestive shots.

Maxim, meanwhile, went for 'Bigger, better, hotter: Billie!' on its June cover over a picture of a wet-haired, apparently naked Billie shielded only by a single palm leaf. Inside, it had bikini shots and a little bit more fun with the palm tree. The tweenie heroine of just a year ago was nowhere to be seen – and both interviews would ultimately cover some seriously suggestive topics.

Two years ago, it had all been about Billie's favourite colour, favourite food and favourite soap star. In the early summer of 2000, when she was still just 17, *Maxim* magazine wanted to know her favourite erogenous zone. And Billie, ever the people pleaser, was happy to tell all – 'Definitely my ears, I like them being gently nibbled. My belly button is also very sensitive and ticklish, which is quite a turn-on, too,' was her perhaps inadvisedly full response. Having answered that question, it would, perhaps, have been asking too much to expect the *Maxim* crew to hold back. So they pushed the sexual envelope even further. 'If you were a bloke, would you be more turned on by a woman's breasts or bum?' they asked. 'I'd go for the arse every time,' Billie responded enthusiastically. 'I hate it when everything's on show. It's so much more exciting when you have to use your imagination and that's always the case with the outline of a nice bum.'

This, of course, led neatly to: 'So, have you seen women in the street and thought, "Mmmm, nice arse"?'

'Yeah, loads of times. Mel B's got one of the greatest arses I have ever seen. Jennifer Lopez and Cindy Crawford have got pretty good butts, too.'

At the time, it all seemed, amazingly, like good clean fun. But a monster had been created by this new promotional campaign. Pre-teen girls were no longer Billie's only target market. Much older men were now in her PR company's sights as well, and the results were never going to be very savoury.

What mattered to Billie, though, was the fact that each article and each set of new pictures had the desired effect. The photos were leaked to the press even before the interviews had been written up and all the newspapers splashed them on their front pages, their page threes and everywhere else they could find.

Unsurprisingly, some of the papers printing the new images claimed that they were only doing so to prove how appalling and exploitative they were. It was promoting jail-bait, some said, the love that dare not speak its age, according to others. But Billie was having none of it. 'I'm old enough to know if someone is trying to exploit me. Men's mags are cool to do sometimes. It's nice to be made to feel sexy and glamorous. Every woman likes that, as long as it is done tastefully.' She also denied the claim that she was being 'sold' to the older men who leered at the lads' mags photos. 'Men don't buy records and they won't start doing so no matter what you look like in a magazine. It just creates a hype, people talk about it and it gets you attention. And, anyway, I'm just getting older, I'm not deliberately going out there and showing off my nipples. It was never a conscious decision like, "Yes! I'm nearly 18. I can be as sexy as I want!" If I feel like wearing something sexy, I'll wear it. I've been away a while. I've changed.'

Regardless of whether these protestations were really true, the fact was that Billie was big news again after nearly a year off the scene. And she was only getting started. Her next trip into infamy came when she headlined at the G.A.Y nightclub in central London. She sang a mix of her old and new hits – and then got a little bit carried away. One moment she was dancing in a catsuit, the next her boobs were on display and on camera. It was a Janet Jackson-style 'wardrobe malfunction' a good five years ahead of its time.

At first, Billie tried to brush the matter aside. 'It has been blown out of all proportion. It was an accident, not me trying to get all raunchy. I was doing a lairy performance because that's what you do there. You're at G.A.Y, everyone's so up for a mad night and it's not like you're performing for men who fancy you, you're performing for men who want you to be completely crazy. I undid my catsuit a bit to reveal my little pink bra but then realised that having not practiced in it, it probably wasn't the best thing to dance around in. It was complete mayhem. I was unaware of what had happened with my breasts.'

Once more, it was great publicity for her new single – which had gone down a storm at G.A.Y. But accidental or not, had the quick flash been a stunt too far? Billie quickly started to see the downsides to her Judy Finnegan moment — not least because some candid shots of her impromptu strip had immediately been sold to the tabloids and had put her back on the front pages in even more revealing fashion. *Sky* magazine reporter Damon Syson was due to meet Billie the morning after the night before at G.A.Y. Bearing in mind, as he said, that 10 million people had been staring at Billie's nipples while eating their breakfast that day, he wasn't convinced that the meeting would go ahead. But it did. And he says Billie was the ultimate professional. 'Warm, confident and totally self-possessed.' But she also admitted she was temporarily mortified.

'I'm hating the idea of walking into shops and having all these blokes sniggering at me and saying, "We've… seen… your…. niiiipples," and thinking it's hilarious. And having pictures of me on the front page of the *Sport* with my tits falling out at a concert? I know it must be shit for my dad down at Jewson's getting his cement. And for my mum picking the kids up from school and maybe nobody wanting to talk to her any more. It must have been terrible for them last year when people would say I was doing coke or having abortions every other week. I sort of stopped reading it, but I knew people were saying stuff and I knew my parents would feel it because they were trying to shield me from it.'

Unfortunately for Billie, an even bigger crisis was just about to hit her, however. Behind the scenes, Ritchie

Neville had supported her throughout all the traumas of the previous year. He had looked after her when she had been ill; he had given her space when she needed rest; he had inspired her to get back to work and to move her career forward when she was ready. The pair even lived together in the £200,000 flat Billie had bought the previous year when she finally tired of living in hotel rooms. But it looked as though Ritchie wasn't going to be around for ever.

Things had come to a head just after Easter when Billie's promotional role started to take over her life once more. Ritchie had been equally busy as 5ive's latest single, 'Don't Wanna Let You Go', hit the shops. And he was also on the road – the group was touring and making promotional appearances across North America with further trips to the Far East planned for the summer. He and Billie were finding it too hard to make time for each other – suddenly, every time Ritchie was in the country, Billie seemed to be abroad and vice-versa. And suddenly this didn't seem to matter as much as it ought to. After 18 great months together, they realised their relationship had come to the end of the line.

The media, however, were not prepared to accept that the pair had just grown apart and were going their separate ways in an adult, amicable fashion. Instead, the headlines claimed Billie had been dumped... by telephone. Both would soon deny this claim, but Billie was clearly struggling with the thought of being alone. 'There were tears and I feel gutted, just numb and heartbroken,' she told the reporters who clamoured for a reaction every time she left the home she and Ritchie had shared. 'I wasn't aware that a split was around the corner. We didn't see a lot of each other and I knew that would take its toll. But I loved him and I thought our love would conquer that. What's worse is that right now I feel as if he is just away and I am just waiting for him to come home. Even when we were apart, I used to speak to him every night before I went to bed and that won't happen any more. That will be the most difficult thing of all to cope with.'

And still the questions came from reporters who had tracked down her home and mobile phone numbers or were waiting to spot her at her record company, management offices or any of the other points around town where they could send their spies. 'You would think nobody else has ever split up before, the way everyone has gone on about this,' she told one reporter, trying to bring closure and a sense of perspective to the situation. 'The relationship was good while it lasted but it is over now. And, luckily, I don't have time to sit down and dwell on it.'

This couldn't have been more true. Having recorded 12 tracks for her new album, Billie had picked the first single, 'Day & Night'. It was due to be released in just two weeks' time. Billie had co-written 'Day & Night' with Eliot Kennedy, Tim Lever and Mark Cawley, all of whom were experts in the mainstream pop market. The lyrics told of a sense of longing, bordering on obsession, and when added to the R&B edge in both Billie's voice and the production, it produced the maturity everyone felt her career required. The bubblegum brunette had disappeared along with her boyfriend. Newly single and fully blonde, she had even re-acquired her surname. Forget the teen-queen Billie; from now on, it was going to be Billie Piper, thank you very much.

The bad news for Billie as she waited for the release date was that her nemesis was already at the top of the charts. Britney was at Number One with what was in a way her comeback single, 'Oops I Did It Again', the first release from her same-named second album. Hitting the top slot had pushed Britney past Billie in the history books – it was her third Number One and she had achieved it at just 18 years, five months and three days old. Would Billie's return to the chart be as successful?

The mid-week sales figures when 'Day & Night' was finally released suggested that it was. The buzz over the single grew over the course of the week and on Sunday, 27 May, Billie got the call she had been hoping for. She, too, had her third Number One record, and saw 'Oops I Did It Again' pushed down to Number Three in the process. What made the story all the sweeter was the fact that at 17 years, 7 months and 23 days old, Billie was almost a year younger than Britney.

Billie's return to form made headlines, the first positive ones she had received in some time. But for all this, her core fans were infuriated at the lack of respect she seemed to generate as an artist. The public perception of her was that she was a lightweight, especially when put up against her American rivals. It seemed that her shortcomings were always being emphasised, and her achievements were never fully recognised. 'There must be some kind of cultural thing where we think any trend or any person that comes over from America is better than anything we can produce at home,' says Miles Davenport, who put together a Billie fansite in 2000. 'Any way you looked at it, Billie's chart record was stronger than Britney's. She hadn't had a million-selling single but, in terms of chart positioning, she had done more and she had done it sooner than anyone else. But still the British media mocked her and built up Britney. I lost count of the times that Billie was referred to in papers as a "wannabe Britney" or a "Britney clone". I even once saw her described as "Britain's low-budget Britney remake". To my mind, it should always have been the other way around because Billie was here first. And, by definition, she has also lasted longer, which is an achievement of its own in something as fickle as the music industry.'

Back at her new flat in Maida Vale, north-west London, Billie was ready to celebrate, however. The girl who had always been terrified of failure had very publicly succeeded again. She was exhausted, but exhilarated. And as she tried to enjoy the moment – something she still regrets she had been unable to do with her first Number One – she found herself forgetting the lessons of her past. She forgot, for example, how fragile she could be when she was tired. She forgot how suddenly her adrenalin rush could dry up and leave her drained and tearful. Most of all, perhaps, she forgot she was still just 17 years old.

Too many late nights followed too many early mornings as Billie temporarily rejoined the breakfast television and Saturday morning TV show circuit. She was also in demand internationally as 'Day & Night' was released across Europe and beyond – and this triggered a particularly bitter dispute over her reliability as a performer. In the spring, she had signed a big budget contract to headline at London's Alexandra Palace as part of a summer concert for University of Greenwich students (who were paying up to £55 a head for the evening). Unfortunately for the organisers, no one had noticed the small print in the contract which said that Billie was obligated to give priority to international publicity – and one week before the concert date, she found out her 'Day & Night' promotional schedule meant she had to appear on French television instead. The girl band Honeyz was drafted in to replace Billie at Ally Pally, but it couldn't stop a war of words between the concert organisers and Billie's management. 'We had even got permission from her parents for her to perform after 11.00pm. It must be after her bedtime,' Student Union manager Paul Hart said caustically, amidst rumours that they wanted to sue for £100,000 over Billie's non-appearance.

The row was widely reported in the press and was

particularly hurtful for Billie because the one thing she was most proud of was her reputation as a work-horse and a professional. While so many other celebrities constantly kept journalists and photographers waiting, Billie prided herself on always trying to be early for her appointments, for example. She talked with her management company about every appearance or job she agreed to take on, believing that once she had agreed to something, it was set in stone. She also paid attention to her travel arrangements, wanting to know there would always be enough time to get from one place to another so she wouldn't keep people waiting and could give her best from the moment she arrived at an engagement.

That's why the small print problem which had caused the problems with the University of Greenwich had genuinely upset her, and the media coverage of the incident was distressing. Several papers took the line that she had grown too big for her boots, feeling a student concert was beneath her after her third Number One. Some also hinted that she was ill again and had been unable to perform for any of the usual made up reasons they had used so many times before.

Depressed, she decided to try and dance her troubles away… which turned out to be the worst possible of ideas.

It was a warm Friday night when Billie headed out on the town with a couple of her dancers and their friends. She had been feeling shattered all day but knew that if she stayed in she would end up stewing over her latest bout of bad press and probably wouldn't sleep well anyway. So she tied her hair back, pulled on some combats and a tight black top and headed into the West End.

The group wanted to go to Bar 38 in Covent Garden, a crowded wine bar that packs out with local office workers and tourists from the early afternoon onwards. By the time Billie and her crowd arrived, just after 9.00pm, it was standing room only but the atmosphere was as buzzy as everyone had hoped. The group found themselves a spot, ordered some drinks and started talking, laughing and dancing a little in the crowd. Then Billie, who had been feeling even worse on her journey into town, suddenly felt a sharp pain in her side. She rushed off to the toilets where she was shocked at how pale she looked in the mirrors. Something was wrong. She pushed her way through the crowds so she could tell her friends she was getting seriously worried – and then she collapsed.

'One minute I was talking to my friends saying I thought I needed to go to hospital, then I had the biggest head rush ever and I collapsed. The next thing I knew, some guy I didn't know just lifted me up and carried me out.'

The man in question, 27-year-old entertainment company boss Adam Clarke, said, 'There was a crowd of us chatting when all of a sudden Billie passed out. I picked her up in my arms and carried her to her car. Her friends told me they would take her to hospital. She seemed to be really ill but I know she hadn't been drinking and I'm pretty sure it wasn't drugs.'

In a west London hospital, the doctors confirmed Clarke's belief. But the papers needed a whole lot more persuading, not least because they found (or invented) a host of unnamed 'onlookers' who said Billie had been 'in and out of the toilet all night', that her eyes had been 'rolling in the back of her head' and that she had been 'foaming at the mouth' while unconscious. Every possible hint at drug abuse that they could make without being sued for libel was made. And Billie fought back.

'This has nothing to do with drugs — I don't do drugs — and there was no foaming of the mouth,' she said from her hospital bed. She was disobeying doctors' orders not to speak to anyone because she knew how important it was to get her side of the story into the open. 'There has been a lot of stuff happening to me over the last couple of months and I think it has all got on top of me. Yes, I collapsed, but there was no sinister reason behind it. It was a whole lot of things. My brain was working overtime because I had just broken up with my boyfriend and I had been working really hard on the single, so I was exhausted. On top of that — and this is a bit embarrassing — I also had really bad cystitis, which was bloody unbelievably painful.'

The doctors said Billie should be kept in hospital at least overnight and her parents drove up from Swindon to be at her bedside. When she was finally allowed home after nearly 48 hours in the hospital, she was prescribed antibiotics and was told she needed total rest for at least another two days and nights. The consultant who had examined her before she was discharged had also diagnosed a second bout of the kidney infection she had first been hit with the previous year. 'I have had this before and it may be a recurring thing when I am run-down and tired. I felt numb and heartbroken about Ritchie. I am still getting used to being on my own after such a long relationship. I was ill and now I am just a bit weak,' she said as she finally prepared to face the world again in late June.

Her mum, Mandy, had meanwhile stocked up her daughter's kitchen and tried to dampen down the rumours that Billie was somehow going off the rails. 'We worry about her a lot, but she's a teenager and she's doing all the usual sorts of things that all teenagers do,' she said. 'As a parent, you hardly ever see your children when they are happy. But you just have to be there when things go bad.'

What Mandy and Paul had proved after Billie's collapse was that they were the right people to have around in a crisis. Billie had found out the hard way that she would always have unconditional love and an unquestioning refuge with her parents should she ever need it.

Over the next few weeks, not all of the healthy food Mandy had put in her daughter's fridge got eaten, though, because Billie had decided to really chill out – and that meant plenty of lazy nights in with a DVD and an Indian takeaway. 'Those are my favourite times. You're not trying to be anyone you're not. Not trying to impress anyone. You're not out being a star. Showbiz parties are naff if you go to them all the time and I'm too young for sex and drugs and rock 'n' roll,' she said. But the media continued to suggest that Billie was indeed in danger of falling for a sex, drugs and rock 'n' roll lifestyle. And plenty of people were queuing up to give her advice.

Sun reporter Dominic Mohan was one of them. 'I watched Billie grow up in front of my eyes,' he said, making the point that he had been the first national newspaper reporter to interview her back in 1998 and had been a firm fan ever since. But in the summer of 2000, Dominic was increasingly worried about the teenager's health — and her future. In an open letter to Billie, published in the newspaper, he wrote:

> *'Billie, something is wrong. A recurring kidney problem at 17 is unusual. Your health is more important than getting up to promote some single or album. Talk to your parents and try to steer clear of the pitfalls of fame and success at such a young age. There are a lot of temptations for a young girl in London's showbiz society. Forget partying hard at the Titanic Bar and Rock as I have seen you doing — you should spend some time with your young friends in Swindon. Get back to your roots and don't throw it all away. I want to be writing about you as the new Queen of Pop and not another showbiz casualty.'*

Unfortunately for Billie, all this was easier said than done. Her trips back to Swindon the previous year had been marred by jeers, insults and even physical violence. All that now seemed to have passed, but having not lived there full time since she was 12, it was hardly going to be easy for Billie to make new friends there. Instead, she chose to focus on her small circle of friends in London. Most of them were quite a few years older than her but, as most of them were in the music world, they at least had more of an idea of what kind of pressure she was under. And Billie was prepared to learn from them.

One of her confidantes at this point was actress-turned-singer Martine McCutcheon who had briefly shared the same record company office. 'Call her Tiffany and you're dead,' is what Billie had been warned before meeting her – adding to the nerves she already felt about talking to one of her *EastEnders* heroines. But as it turned out, the pair got on like a house on fire. At 24, Martine was seven years older than Billie and was happy to take on the role of the big sister Billie had never had, one who knew all the ins and outs of the entertainment industry and who had had first-hand experience of the excesses of the tabloid press.

'She gives me loads of advice and I love her attitude... I love the fact that she doesn't take any crap from anyone,' Billie said of her new mentor. The pair certainly had plenty in common: both had been at Number One in the charts, yet both had been relentlessly mocked by music critics and record reviewers; both had suffered their fair share of bad relationships; and both were prone to over-work, exhaustion and illness, as Martine would soon prove in her troubled run as Eliza Doolittle in *My Fair Lady*.

In August 2000, Billie was back on the road and in the air. She was booked to make her second appearance of the year on the BBC's Saturday morning children's magazine show *FBi*. The show, hosted by Vernon Kay, Kate Heavenor and former Boyzone singer Keith Duffy, was filmed in Glasgow and, immediately after her appearance, Billie was scheduled to perform at a summer festival just outside the city.

After returning to London, she was booked to fly to France for the first of a series of performances across Europe before heading to do more of the same in North America. 'Day & Night' was still being rolled out across the world and the second single from her still unreleased second album was due out in Britain in less than a month, so the promotional pressure was on.

Billie was struggling to keep up, however. Her insomnia was back and the more she worried about having the energy for all her live appearances, the more sleepless nights she seemed to suffer. And after performing on *FBi,* being interviewed, photographed and signing autographs, it all came to a head. She headed backstage to the dressing room, felt the now familiar shooting pains in her stomach and abdomen and collapsed. The house doctor examined her, her festival gig was cancelled and she was booked on to the first flight back to London. A car picked her up at Heathrow and she was driven to a private doctor in Harley Street.

He confirmed that Billie's kidney complaint was back with a vengeance – and that she must have been in agony when she fainted.

The diagnosis was pretty much the same as it had been earlier in the year. Billie had to drink plenty of water to flush out her system, and in future had to try and keep herself hydrated whenever she felt under pressure. The trip to the Continent was cancelled as she had a few days' rest at her flat. But beyond that, it had to be business as usual.

At the end of the week, a still-pale Billie was driven back to Heathrow for her scheduled flight to Canada. Already, the treadmill was turning – and while Billie was singing for her supper in North America, plenty of people were still worrying about her back at home. Julia Dickinson, the drama teacher who had effectively launched Billie's road to fame by encouraging her to apply to the Sylvia Young Theatre School in London, was one of them. 'There is a now such a great burden on Billie to succeed,' she said. 'She clearly knows she has to appeal to a wider age group and has to appear grown-up both on and off stage. She obviously needs time to relax and calm down but I am sure whenever there are problems there will be pressure on her to get back to work as soon as possible. If someone is not in the limelight for a while, they are soon forgotten about. I am very worried about her, very concerned. She needs to be allowed to be a normal girl again. I think people forget how young she is.'

While Julia was genuinely trying to help Swindon's biggest export (and had remained in touch with Billie and her family all her life), other locals seemed to be crying crocodile tears about her sudden vulnerability. Several supposed former friends took advantage of the worries over Billie's health to offer new kiss-and-tell stories to the papers. 'She is very emotional now, very much on the edge. Everyone thinks Billie is having a great time because she is a pop star, but she has got a rough life for a girl of her age. She is under so much stress that she sometimes says she has had enough of the TV shows and interviews, promotions, gigs and tours. The bottom line is that she is exhausted. Billie loves being famous but she cries to me a lot. In many ways, she longs to be normal again,' claimed one former friend amidst many other uncorroborated stories.

When Billie got back to Britain and read some of the latest exposés, she was sanguine, rather than angry. The truth was that she was still too tired to feel anything very deeply. 'They are dropping like flies, my friends, with every record I release,' she said, with heart-breaking honesty. She had tried hard to turn her London flat into a proper home, but said she was too afraid ever to take many people back to see it – and this was compounding her long-standing sense of loneliness. 'I have to be really choosy about the people I invite back there. I can't trust a lot of people. I don't like the thought of anyone snooping about, so unfortunately I can't be an amazing hostess. That side of this business is the small print I didn't read when I signed the contract,' she said, her voice tailing off as she described how isolated her life had suddenly become.

Billie was also becoming increasingly frustrated about the way her every action could be twisted by the media – so she couldn't do right for doing wrong. 'I go out and try and do normal things because I don't want to reach 30 and be insecure and lonely and feel I have missed out on my life,' she said, quite reasonably. 'But I can't win because, if I do go out, then I am made out to be some kind of a wild child and people think everything I am drinking is alcoholic, when it isn't. I'm actually a very responsible person. I run my own life, I do my own cooking, washing and cleaning. I also work very hard and people never get to see that.'

Amidst so much press interest, even the most ordinary of incidents were blown out of all proportion. Billie had to abandon a headline appearance at a Radio One Roadshow in Cornwall when her flight was cancelled and there was no other way to get to the venue in time, for example. But the following day, the papers screamed that Billie's flight had needed to divert to a different airport after extreme turbulence had left Billie 'terrified and shaken'. It had been a 'near-death experience' for everyone on board, the report stated. 'But I never even got on the plane,' Billie said. It had never taken off, let alone had an emergency landing.

The good news for Billie as the pressure mounted in her personal life was that her next single was earning some good pre-release reviews. 'Something Deep Inside' was described as 'addictive', 'musically credible' and 'a cracking pop song with more than a hint of R&B'. She certainly looked confident on the CD sleeve – wearing a white vest, she was the perfectly tanned gap-year girl, posing on a beach with an old straw hat pulled down over her holiday blonde hair.

Taking 'Something Deep Inside' to the top of the charts was always going to be a challenge, though. She was competing with the Mariah Carey and Westlife duet 'Against All Odds', plus singles from Pink, Green Day and Anastacia, whose song 'I'm Outta Love' had already been a huge hit in America and around the world. Billie, though, had two extra reasons for wanting to do well with 'Something Deep Inside'. First, she had co-written it with Eliot Kennedy and Tim Woodcock, so felt a stronger sense of ownership and pride in it. Second, if it did well, it would be the perfect 18th birthday present – and as the single's release date approached, it was looking as if Billie's big birthday was going to be a massive disappointment.

In happier days, the idea had been for the party to be a joint one with Ritchie, whose birthday fell very close to hers. When that plan had fallen through with the end of their relationship, Billie had taken on all the organisation herself. And when the big night came, it compounded all her biggest insecurities. It also reminded her of all the reasons why she was finding it hard to be happy.

The first problem was a feeling that what should have been a perfect night for Billie's family and friends seemed to have been hijacked by the music industry. The party, at Soho club Papa Gaio, was also being used as the joint launch night for 'Something Deep Inside' and Billie's second album, *Walk of Life*. The press were there in force and, in order to create some atmosphere and keep them happy, Billie's management had laid on plenty of rent-a-celebrity guests. As Billie looked around the room, she realised that she knew very few of the people there. Admittedly, several of the famous faces there had become friends over the past few years, especially fellow singers like Kerry Katona, H from Steps and television presenter Katy Hill. But what about all the former *Big Brother* contestants and other so-called famous names? Billie had no idea why they were there. And it seemed desperately sad that she needed them to fill out a room. 'In the music industry, not everyone is your friend,' she had said, sadly, when she had been ill earlier in the year. Now she seemed to have precious few alternative friends to call upon for support. It was her 18th birthday, but she suddenly felt totally alone and utterly adrift from the proceedings.

The final straw, which nearly caused a fight, was that other people saw Billie's 18th birthday party as a chance to take a pot shot at her or laugh at her expense. A reporter from the *Sun*, for example, tried to get into the club with a sniffer dog the paper claimed was called Charlie. The hope, presumably, was that the dog would find cocaine or other drugs in the venue and 'expose' the story in the next day's paper. To Billie, it seemed a desperately cruel and depressing stunt and, when she found out about it, her first instinct had been to cancel the whole evening and head off home.

The one person who stopped her from doing so was Ritchie Neville. He proved himself to be one of the good guys by turning up at the party and persuading his ex-girlfriend to put a brave face on things. He said he could tell just how distracted and upset she seemed to be from the moment he arrived, so he dragged her on to the dance floor to try and take her mind off all the reporters and the hangers-on. He just wanted her to have a good time and flash the big wide smile he had fallen in love with what seemed like half a lifetime ago.

Unfortunately, the following day things seemed to get worse rather than better for Billie. The early pre-release reviews of 'Something Deep Inside' had been replaced by some savage post-release alternatives. So the mid-week sales figures were not expected to make pleasant reading.

One paper called Billie 'the cut-and-paste queen of pop' and accused her of 'stealing shamelessly' from Britney et al – another example of the kind of skewed comment which fan Miles Davenport had despaired of earlier in the summer. 'Sadly, her Jill-of-all-Trades magpie habits result in something less interesting than the sum of its pop-picking parts. Billie has to realise it takes more than dressing up in borrowed clothes to turn heads and get feet stomping,' was another sniffy review of the new single.

When Sunday came and the chart countdown was over, Mariah Carey and Westlife were in the Number One slot and 'Something Deep Inside' had peaked at Number Four. Getting into the Top Five yet again was a huge achievement, but for Billie it felt like something of a failure.

Three days after the chart was unveiled, Billie flew out to South-East Asia for a round of appearances there — Japan was also on her list as a territory to consolidate with an extended visit later in the year. And before then she had a series of meetings about a new assault on America and a full-scale British tour.

'I don't just want to be a hit in the UK. I want to be as famous as Madonna.' That's what a younger, less cynical and more open Billie Piper had said as little as 12 months earlier. In the autumn of 2000, though, world domination could hardly have been further from her mind. Still, she agreed to a series of new appearances in America towards the end of the year. However little she wanted to go, she was very aware of her responsibilities to Innocent and all the people who worked for her. She wanted the company to get a decent return on its financial investment and she wanted to pay it back for the faith it had shown in her throughout all her bad days. At first, it also seemed as if going abroad might be a good idea if it took the heat off Billie in the UK. She could hardly have done more to promote *Walk of Life*, her second album, but sales just weren't picking up. Just after her birthday, it had entered the album charts at just Number 14 – and it didn't seem to be a climber. Innocent was still talking about a UK tour for the spring, and they had plans to release at least two more singles to try and give the album another lease of life. But, so far, things weren't looking good.

As a trickle of newspaper columnists started to hint that Billie's career was on the skids, others weighed in with the mockery. A 13-year-old girl from Newport on the Isle of Wight had just been in court accused of mugging a pensioner so she could afford a ticket to a Billie Piper concert the previous year, for example. What would be a suitable punishment for doing the same in 2000, the writers asked? Forcing the girl to listen to Billie's latest album, they joked.

For Billie, the biggest issue as she struggled with the poor sales figures and low-level criticism wasn't that her own ego was hurting. She had finally accepted that having had three Number One singles she had nothing more to prove in the pop world. What mattered instead was the feeling that she had somehow let other people down by not setting the world alight with the album. She felt some kind of responsibility to everyone she worked with, all the people who had made such huge efforts on the project. She was embarrassed that she was no longer producing the results that they were hoping for. And so, in spite of herself, she agreed to the next big promotional push. And it was then that the cracks really began to show.

She was in America, on one occasion supporting

Jennifer Lopez and singing in front of a stadium full of 100,000 fans – including President Clinton. But as the mini-tour continued, she was overcome with doubts. 'I was in Chicago and it suddenly dawned on me that I didn't want to be there doing this. It petrified me. I thought, "What else am I going to do?" And I thought, "I'm going to have to let some people down." I'm a massive people-pleaser and didn't want to hurt anyone.' She also felt a sudden burst of guilt. 'I was thinking, I know so many kids at stage school who are desperate to be pop stars. And here I am thinking I don't want to do this.'

Flying home, having told nobody about her dramatic change of heart, Billie felt her mood harden. When she got back to London, she decided to start partying – hard. Looking back, she says she is fiercely proud that through all her turmoil she never missed a single professional engagement. But she was certainly looking for something new in the evenings. She wanted to have fun. 'I think I was just starting to get quite rebellious,' is how she explains it. 'I was never a diva, it is not in my nature to throw tantrums at work or at home. But all this was just my way of saying I needed some control over my life. It was a slow build but I was getting more and more frustrated. Everybody had their hands on me.

'I felt cheated because I felt I was the only person getting nothing out of it all – but I was so tired I stopped caring. You start beating yourself down and you don't have the energy. Everyone and everything suffers, so I would go out and get hammered. It sounds much more dramatic than it was. I didn't do it for long and it was only once a month.'

But however recently the drinking bouts had started, and however infrequently they took place, they soon acquired legendary status in the media.

Billie's new 'party girl' tag seemed to have stuck. But one journalist saw something else behind the façade. Kate Thornton, a *Sunday Times* writer long before becoming the *X-Factor* presenter, was the first to have a real insight into what was going on. 'Behind the confident and sunny disposition, there is something infinitely sad about Billie Piper which she desperately tries to conceal,' said Kate, genuinely worried about the surprisingly tiny girl she had just spent an afternoon getting to know.

And this sadness extended to the whole Piper family. Billie told Kate that she had only just started to become aware of how her lifestyle had affected her parents and disrupted her friendships with her brother and sister. 'I suddenly looked back and could see it must have been hard for my parents right back from when I went to Sylvia Young's. How hard it was for them to accept that their child was no longer at home, was no longer all theirs. My mother missed that teenage life with me which I suddenly found terribly sad.' It felt, suddenly, as if Billie had given up too much in return for her pop career.

But what could she do about it?

As autumn deepened, Billie decided not to give in to

the depression she could feel creeping up all around her. Instead, she vowed to change her life completely. She had done so before; she could do so again. At this point, on a weekend back in Swindon, she bumped into a group of older people from her first ever drama class in the town. They were at university, and amidst talk of eating baked beans out of tins and re-using tea bags (the two things Billie had thought all students did, and which her friends assured her were simply not the case) she had fallen in love with the idea of a world where you could sit anonymously in the college bar all night with nothing more to worry about than a late essay or an early lecture. She had no illusion that she too wanted to do a degree, but she admired the fact that her friends were thriving at their various colleges. And somehow this seemed to inspire her to reinvent her own life in a similar fashion.

At this stage, Billie had absolutely no time-frame in mind for the transformation. Neither had she worked out what she wanted to do next. But she felt better from the moment that she made the decision to change things. Keeping that decision a secret helped as well. For the first time in many years, Billie felt in control of her own destiny; she felt powerful again, because she knew something that no one else even suspected.

Innocent had decided that her next single would be the 'Walk of Life' title track from her album, and that once more Billie would be going for a Christmas Number One. Having just turned on the Regent Street Christmas lights alongside London Mayor Ken

Livingstone, Billie was prepared to admit that she might be in with a chance. She liked 'Walk of Life', and she was prepared to do all the usual hard work to get everyone else to like it as well.

Competition for the Christmas Number One slot was typically tough, though, with both Kylie Minogue and Robbie Williams due to release singles on the same day. But Billie was ready to throw herself wholeheartedly into her bid to beat them. The idea of quitting while she was winning seemed hugely attractive. So she wanted that Christmas Number One spot all the more keenly.

As her natural competitiveness came back to the fore, so, too, did her energy. Early-morning television shows suddenly seemed like a breeze; newspaper and magazine interviews were a pleasure. And she jumped at the chance to do some high-profile radio shows. One of the ones she was looking forward to the most was the Virgin Radio breakfast show, one of the most popular and the funniest in the country. Its host was Chris Evans.

5
HELLO, CHRIS

IT STARTED WITH a hug. It was 13 December 2000, and Billie had arrived at the Golden Square studios of Virgin Radio to join the banter on the *Chris Evans Breakfast Show*. As usual, she was early, so she had plenty of time to say hello to Chris and his team before the show went on air.

Chris noticed that the rest of his crew and producers got handshakes or kisses on the cheek as Billie introduced herself to everyone in the studio. But when it came to his turn, he noticed something different. 'When she arrived, she gave me a hug which seemed a bit too tight and I thought, "Hang on, that wasn't the usual showbiz hug... what was all that about?"' he says. And he admits he was being hyper-sensitive about everything Billie said or did that day, because he had been hugely looking forward to seeing her again.

He had read almost everything that had been written about Billie since they had first met on *TFI Friday* earlier in the year, and while he knew most of it was probably nonsense, he was worried that the young, sparky girl he had liked so much was in trouble. He knew – perhaps better than anyone – how sudden fame and fortune can bring problems as well as advantages. And he wondered if there was any way he could help her cope with the way her world was changing.

The other reason Chris had followed Billie's career was much simpler– he liked her. And he hadn't been shy about telling this to his friends. Chef and restaurateur Aldo Zilli was one of them. He and Chris had been drinking partners for years and he was the first person to spot that romance might be in the air that December. 'I had lunch with Chris one day in early December and happened to mention that I had bumped into Billie Piper the night before,' says Aldo. 'I have never seen him so excited about anyone. He said to me, "I hope you got her number." Unfortunately, I hadn't. A week later, though, Billie was booked on to his breakfast show to promote her new single. I was also there, cooking, and the chemistry between them was electric.'

That chemistry made itself clear in one of the funniest breakfast shows Chris had hosted in some time. He and Billie sparked off each other from the start, even when Chris joked about whether his guest might get back together with and ultimately marry Ritchie Neville. Just as they had done on *TFI Friday*, the pair complemented each other on their choice of clothes and, once more, they swapped shirts on air (though as stunts go, this one wasn't quite as effective on radio). At one point during the show, Billie asked Chris to come to the *Smash Hits!* party with her the following evening and Chris even jokingly asked her to marry him. The whole team seemed on a roll, the breakfast slot seemed to fly past and, as far as Chris was concerned, he was hooked. 'That was the start of it, really. It became clear very quickly that there was a connection between us and a real mutual respect,' he says. That and a whole lot of flirting.

After the show, there were more handshakes and kisses on the cheeks for the team and another close hug between Billie and Chris. With no prompting from Aldo, Chris finally made sure he and Billie had each other's numbers before she waved him a last goodbye. He then had a busy day and a long night ahead. It was the day of the Ginger Media Group's big Christmas party, being held at Aldo's Zilli's flagship restaurant in Soho. Under normal circumstances, that would have meant everything else being forgotten. But Billie didn't seem to be someone he could forget. Chris hardly drank, couldn't really focus and finally made his apologies and left the party uncharacteristically early. He had called Billie's mobile and wanted to take her out to dinner. Neither saw the meal as a date but a whole lot more flirting went on. Something good was certainly in their air.

The following night was even busier. Billie performed 'Walk of Life' on *Top of the Pops*, feeling like a veteran on the show as her appearances there approached double figures. She then wanted to take Chris to the *Smash Hits!* party as she had told listeners on the breakfast show, and the pair then took in Denim and Brown's in a long night of club and bar hopping.

At the first party of the night, Billie even dragged an unwilling Chris on to the dancefloor. 'She told me I was a good dancer – or at least she gave me 10 out of 10 for effort,' Chris said the next day when he woke hungover just before the start of his breakfast show.

To return the favour the following evening, he took Billie to his favourite pub, the Nag's Head in Knightsbridge. Small, cosy and traditional, the pub is like a country local, somehow transplanted in the golden streets of Belgravia near Harrods and Hyde Park. Famous for its beers and its bar staff, there are plenty of quiet tables for couples who don't want to be disturbed. And that was exactly how Billie and Chris felt on what was effectively their third date. The pair huddled together all evening, talking intensely and periodically laughing out loud. Billie and Chris turned out to have huge amounts to say to each other. Both admitted that they sometimes felt like anything from aliens to frauds in the upper levels of the entertainment universe. Both said they sometimes couldn't work out how their lives had gone from the ordinary to the extraordinary at such speed. And both agreed that sometimes they felt their careers were racing ahead out of their own control.

In the months and years ahead, rumours would

abound about how much the pair both drank. But that first evening in the Nag's Head, it really didn't seem too much of a cliché to say that they were drunk on each other. For Billie, every extra hour she spent with Chris confirmed how much she liked him. It felt as if a lifetime had passed since she had met someone who seemed to connect so well with her. The more they talked, the more she still seemed to have to say. 'I thought things began to bloom when I went on Chris's show, but I didn't know then if what I felt was for real,' says Billie. 'But I knew he made me laugh like no one ever has before and that is incredibly important.'

With so much going so well, Billie and Chris hardly needed any encouragement to spend more time together. And for Billie, plenty more nights at the Nag's Head would have been a wonderful way to see out the year and build foundations for the future. But when the person you are on the point of dating is a Tarzan-a-gram-turned-media mogul, then you should perhaps expect some grand gestures. Chris certainly had some tricks up his sleeve when it came to wooing, and the first of them was displayed, in spectacular fashion, just three days later. He bought Billie a £105,000 Ferrari.

The car was truly stunning. Chris had chosen a silver 360 Modena – one of the newest in the Ferrari range with an all-aluminium body and a top speed of 295 mph. But even this wasn't enough for the romantic in Chris. After leaving the HR Owen dealership in Kensington, west London, he went shopping for nearly £250 worth of red roses and balloons. He then headed north, parked outside Billie's flat, put the flowers and balloons on the driver's seat and knocked on Billie's front door. He had put the keys in an envelope with a note. The only thing he hadn't done was check whether or not Billie could drive. He would soon find out that she couldn't — indeed, that she hadn't even got around to applying for her provisional licence, let alone having any lessons.

'Why did I give Billie the Ferrari? Because I can. Simple as that. There was no other reason,' was how Chris explained the gift when the media found out about it later that day. 'I have bought cars for people before, but never one this expensive. I didn't have anything to do that day, so I thought I would buy a car. Basically, I could afford it. I thought she would like it and life is about having a laugh. And that was that.'

If nothing else, Chris says Billie's reaction to what ranked as the country's best early Christmas present made the £105,000 list price money well spent. 'It was the funniest thing you have ever seen. I just dropped the keys off at her flat with the note. I then hid behind a garden wall and she came out with her mate. And I am not joking, her face was classic. I wish I had filmed it. She couldn't believe it, but she is happy. The only thing is she can't get the immobiliser off so is in a bit of a panic about that.'

Friends said that while Chris's generosity should never come as a surprise, there was obviously something else going on in his fledgling relationship with Billie. Something very good indeed. Long-term colleague and friend Simon Morris says he was well aware of just how much Chris was hoping to find a true soulmate. 'Chris and I used to talk about looking for love and how it was something he really wanted to find. He always envied that I loved my wife, Helen, and was definitely looking for something that would last.

'I met him by chance in London on the day he bought Billie the Ferrari. This guy on a moped pulled up alongside me in my car and, when the visor came up, I realised it was Chris. He had been driving around the West End on his own, quite obviously high on life. He took his helmet off and simply said, "Si, I've found my Helen," which I thought was wonderful news and a wonderful way to express it.'

For her part, Billie was at a loss for words as she sat in her flat knowing a wildly expensive Ferrari was now parked outside. 'When he bought me the car, I was stunned, it was like something out of a film,' she says. 'I have no idea what I am going to do with it because I can't drive. I sat in it, though, and had a glass of champagne. It was a lovely, lovely thing for him to do.' And if Chris had bought the car to try and push his relationship with Billie forward then it worked – it practically fast-forwarded it. 'Amazingly enough, I really did think back then, "I'm going to marry this guy," says Billie. 'Not because of what the car was or how much it cost, but because I thought, "I want to get to know somebody who does something like this." It was a huge statement and I admired the man who had made it.'

The only problem, potentially, was that when it came to dating younger pop stars, Chris did have form. Little more than a year earlier, he had enjoyed a brief but hugely public relationship with former Spice Girl Geri Halliwell. Geri, at that time, had been promoting her single 'Lift Me Up' and had been desperate to see it beat former Spice colleague Emma Bunton's release to the Number One spot. Billie, when she met Chris, had been promoting 'Walk of Life' and was hoping to get the same success. So it was easy to see why so many people thought this was just another publicity stunt.

Behind the scenes, Chris's close friends could tell that it was something very different, however. And when he spoke to the media, he was in uncharacteristically restrained form, which clearly suggested he was serious about things for a change. 'Billie is ace, a top woman and I have high hopes for this relationship. We are not an item yet, but we went out last night and I am seeing her again tonight. I don't know what is going on, to be honest, but it is very nice and very enjoyable. I've read all the stuff about this being a stunt and it is not the first time that people have said that about me. I didn't take any notice before and I don't take any notice now. I really feel that this is something special,' was all he would say as news of the fledgling relationship started to dominate the papers.

At the end of the week, Billie got some bad news. 'Walk of Life' had only made it to Number 24 in the charts, easily her lowest placing so far. The papers were suddenly full of stories of 'crisis talks' at Innocent and the end of Billie's career. But, for once, Billie herself was able to take it all in her stride. She knew she had done everything in her power to produce a great single and had then worked the promotion as hard as ever. If it was any consolation, Kylie and Robbie were also missing out on the Number One spot – Bob the Builder with 'Can We Fix It?' beat everyone in 2000, an unusual year when the Beatles were suddenly back as the Christmas Number One in the album charts with *One*. So Billie knew she could survive. Countless other singers have recovered from such temporary failures in the past, not least her long-standing idol Madonna. There were still several other great tracks on the album which could be released as singles, and all of that could wait until the New Year, Billie decided. She had other things to focus on, for a change. And she was feeling good about things.

On Christmas Day, Billie opened presents with her family in Swindon. She then headed 90 miles south-east to be with Chris in Godalming, Surrey. The moment she walked through his door at Hascombe Court, their relationship moved up a gear – with a big kiss being his equivalent of her extended hug at the start of the Virgin breakfast show. 'As soon as I arrived, he planted a kiss on me to confirm "This is the reason why you're here and I do like you". It was our first real kiss,' Billie says.

For his part, Chris was just thrilled and flattered to see her. 'Simply the fact that she came so far on Christmas

Day made it clear that something special was happening. And since then we haven't spent a single moment apart. Not a moment,' he said.

The pair got on a plane the following day for the first of their many holidays. But the location of this first trip certainly raised eyebrows. They were staying in a £360-a-night room at the Savoy Hotel on the island of Madeira. And while the hotel itself has a fantastic reputation for relaxed luxury, the island itself isn't exactly racy. Madeira has always been a favourite of the Saga crowd – Billie and Chris reckoned they were among the few hotel guests under the age of 65.

It didn't seem to be very different when they headed elsewhere on the tiny island. In the beach-side Formula One bar, they were the only two people on the dance floor, and then the only two people in the bar full stop. The owner finally asked them if they didn't mind leaving because he wanted to close early and go home to watch television.

Two days into the trip, and the age profile of the hotel guests changed dramatically. What seemed like an entire planeload of British journalists and photographers had descended on the island in search of what was still being seen as the most unlikely couple in showbusiness. Chris, having a wonderful time, threw caution to the wind and talked freely to several of the reporters. He had got to know many of them well during his time in the public eye and was even happy to show off his room to one of the *News of the World* writers. 'We haven't slept together... yet,' he told him. 'But we're sharing this room and snogging each other's lips off.'

After that, perhaps unsurprisingly, it all became a bit tacky. After Billie and Chris had checked out, a group of reporters and photographers made their way back into the room they had just vacated. 'The room is normally used by people who have just got married. We know it is our most romantic room and always use it as the honeymoon suite. Most of our suites have two beds in them, but in Room 317, where Mr Evans was booked in, there is just one large bed,' an unnamed 'hotel source' told the *Sun*. It got worse. 'Mr Evans and his Billie must have been having a good time – yes?' is what the hotel's chambermaid told reporters as she pointed to the crumpled sheets on the double bed the couple had just vacated – crumpled sheets which, of course, needed to be photographed and published in the following day's papers. And as if that wasn't enough, one paper also photographed some 'saucy undies' that it claimed Billie had bought at Ann Summers just before leaving on the trip. The *Sun* topped it all off with a phone poll so readers could vote on whether Billie should stay with Chris or get back together with Ritchie Neville. More than seven out of ten voted for Ritchie.

Oblivious to it all, the pair at the centre of the media storm walked hand in hand through Heathrow on the way back from Madeira – both smiling broadly.

Relationship experts say 'first holiday syndrome' is a big test of a new partnership, and Billie and Chris seemed to have passed with flying colours. But two new tests were just around the corner. First, Chris was going to meet Billie's parents. He had already spoken to them both on the phone and, after hearing so much about them from Billie, he says he felt he knew them pretty well already. But even so, the first real meeting was always going to be nerve-wracking. The DJ and television presenter who had performed in front of millions knew that this was going to be one of his toughest audiences yet.

He and Billie headed over to Swindon on New Year's Day and, as it turned out, everything went well – Chris and Billie's dad Paul even did the washing up together after dinner, which gave them a chance to talk for even longer. Billie, meanwhile, was simply pleased that everyone had got on. 'Dad is a big Chris Evans fan but he wanted to talk to him face to face to make sure I was being looked after. They got on great, had a good chat and Dad and Mum are both just happy for me,' Billie said after the tense first meeting had ended.

The second test for the relationship was far more sobering. Chris had recently befriended a cystic fibrosis sufferer he had met through the Make a Wish Foundation. Debbie Curran was seriously ill, and Chris saw the 16-year-old in hospital in London after returning from Madeira, and then invited her and her mother to join him and Billie in Surrey for a short break. Billie and Debbie got on well, not least because they were so close in age. After undergoing transplant surgery the following week, everyone had hoped that Debbie would make a full recovery, but tragically she died within a month. Billie and Chris joined her mother and family in Ireland for the funeral, holding hands throughout and silently proving that their relationship was founded on more than just a simple love of the good life.

Having flown over so many early hurdles, Billie was becoming uncharacteristically effusive about how much Chris was inspiring and energising her – and how little she now seemed to care about other people's opinions. After dating for nearly two months, cynics still said the relationship was a sham and Billie was ready to put them right. 'Chris is so bright… he is constantly educating himself, seeing things and seeking things. And when I met him, I stopped caring what other people thought. I can honestly say, hand on heart, that this is for real. And it's fun. Chris makes me feel happy and good about myself and surely that is all that matters. He understands the problems of being in our business but he also understands so much more. Chris loves life and I love that attitude. He also understands me, in a way I don't think any other boyfriend ever has.'

It was the first time Billie had used the word 'boyfriend' in public about Chris. And with it, another milestone was crossed.

His friends, meanwhile, needed absolutely no convincing that the super-fast love affair was genuine. 'I have known Chris a long time and I have never seen him so besotted,' said colleague and friend Ian Goddard.

Kevin Lygo, Director of Programmes at Channel Five and a long standing friend of Chris, agreed. 'It is a very special relationship and there is definitely something really big going on between them. Chris is as settled and as happy as I have ever known him. Billie is great and a really good influence on his life.'

What bothered the critics and the cynics was the age gap between the couple. At 34, Chris was almost twice Billie's age and had a daughter from a previous relationship who was only four years younger than Billie. To many commentators, all this was an unsavoury mess and a sign that the couple would never go the distance. But to Billie and Chris, it was irrelevant. Sure, the fact was that some 16 years separated them, but the truth was that they simply didn't feel it. Billie, of course, had already crammed more into her 18 years than most people twice her age, and staying young was one of Chris's key life goals. 'The age difference doesn't bother us in the slightest,' he said. 'Billie is a lot older and wiser than her years and I am a lot younger, so we kind of meet in the middle and it works. She has a very old head on a very lovely body.'

Aldo Zilli confirmed his friend's view. He had now spent plenty of time with the couple and was convinced their love affair had firm foundations. 'The best thing about their relationship is that they became good friends first. She loves him very much, as he does her. Everyone goes on about the age gap between them but it doesn't matter as Chris can be as old or as young as he wants. I should know. Many times I have felt like his son. I have also felt like his father, when he needs looking after.'

The sentiments were repeated by several other friends who said, not always joking, that as far as the age gap was concerned, it was Chris rather than Billie who had some growing up to do if the relationship was to survive.

In the meantime, the pair were just going to have some fun. Billie was on a lull before deciding on her next single. Chris finished work long before midday, so with time on their hands and money in their pockets, they wanted to take advantage of everything London had to offer. As a laugh, Chris invited Billie to join him one night at Stringfellow's. Not surprisingly, it was the first time that Billie had been to the club, but it turned out to be a brilliant evening. The thrill of being somewhere totally unlikely and not a little bit risqué felt like a real release for Billie and the pair were soon befriended by owner Peter Stringfellow and became regular guests – in a few months' time, Billie even footed the bill for a group of dancers to 'serenade' her boyfriend for a 35th birthday present. Perhaps less surprisingly, they also became regulars at the media's favourite Groucho Club in Soho. Once through the revolving door of the private members' club, Billie and Chris felt they could sink into the sofas and lose themselves in the dark, warm interiors.

Despite its glitzy, celebrity-stuffed reputation, one of the other things which Billie and Chris both liked about the Groucho Club was the fact that it didn't seem to matter what you wore there. Chris wasn't exactly famous for his fashion sense, and Billie was suddenly finding it an enormous relief simply to pull on a pair of combat trousers and a big baggy shirt for an evening out, rather than dressing up to the nines in full pop star regalia. As far as she was concerned, grunge was good — and as she proved it, she unwittingly gave the papers even more ammunition to use against her.

The latest attack was based on what commentators saw as her grim new image. She and Chris might not have been going out for very long, but as they were temporarily Britain's most photographed couple, there were plenty of pictures to illustrate any features on Billie's sartorial decline. Images of her looking glossy and glamorous on a magazine shoot six months earlier were printed alongside the latest examples of her leaving pubs and clubs in the early hours. It wasn't a fair comparison, but a new mythology had been born of a supposedly hard-drinking, low-living Billie who was once again risking her health and threatening to throw her career away. 'Billie Piper and Chris Evans are going out... but only as far as the pub,' was one of the more light-hearted descriptions of their new lifestyle. Jonathan Ross found it equally hard to resist a dig at the new celebrity coupling. 'Billie can't be here tonight because she is going to the cash machine. Or, as I prefer to call him, Chris Evans,' he joked, when hosting the British Comedy Awards to one of the biggest laughs of the night.

But while many others were far less sympathetic, Billie had finally become able to shake off and ignore all the negative comments and the criticisms. The jokes and the jibes were temporarily water off a duck's back. She knew her parents and those closest to her were aware of how happy and grounded she was with Chris. So she carried on doing what she wanted, even though this would end up making things even worse.

Matters came to a head on the second Friday of February when Billie and Chris had another big night out. It began with a meal at the Zilli Fish Too restaurant in the West End, although they seemed to end up drinking a little more than they ate. They then hit the Groucho Club, popped into one other crowded Soho pub, before despairing of the queue at the bar and heading to the Midas Touch bar two doors down from Virgin Radio. Over the course of the evening, Chris was estimated to have sunk ten pints of beer, Billie ten halves – a lot, but no more than many other loved-up Friday night revellers in the West End.

What made the evening stand out was that when Billie and Chris decided to leave their final bar of the evening, she tripped over a bag on the floor, stumbled, felt dizzy and ended up on the ground. Chris sobered up fast and got a glass of water for her from the bar and an embarrassed Billie was soon being led out into the fresh air. Again, it was no more than would happen to countless other people across the capital that night. But Billie's 'drunken collapse' was once more to make headline news – and those who knew her were getting increasingly worried.

David Calder, her former drama teacher at Swindon's

Bradon Forest comprehensive, was one of them. 'It is like watching a mouse on a motorway. She has no idea of how to survive all this attention,' he said. Calder's thoughts on his former pupil's love affair with Chris Evans were even starker. 'I don't think I am alone in thinking the whole spectacle is quite obscene. She is just a child. Billie has become a product, not a person. I don't recognise the nice, bubbly kid I saw at school and I am not sure her parents would either. Children should be allowed to grow up as children. Billie was robbed of her childhood.'

Calder had supported his pupil when she auditioned for the Sylvia Young Theatre School just after starting at Bradon Forest; he wished her well as she headed off to London and kept in touch ever since. But he feared she was now being badly advised — if she was being advised at all. 'People peddle this myth that you only get one shot at success and that you have to take the chance when it comes. But it just isn't true. If you have real talent, you can bide your time. I just hope Billie can pull through the next couple of years and come out of it as her own person. Children need protection from the entertainment industry but often they don't get it. I am keeping my fingers crossed for Billie.'

Another former insider to flag up her worries was Molly Tanner, the principal of the Tanwood Dance School and casting agency in Swindon which taught Billie her first real lessons and got the nine-year-old her first professional jobs. 'Billie has done brilliantly so far and she has done it on her own, not on the back of anyone else,' Molly said. 'So I don't see what she can see in Chris Evans and why she is not with someone more her own age. I don't know if she really knows what is going on. She probably thinks it is all just a great adventure.'

Ritchie Neville's mother Kim Dolphin was equally concerned. 'She used to be so innocent but now she is totally different. She has changed completely since she met Chris Evans,' Kim said of the girl she had once thought might become her daughter-in-law. Billie's drinking, Kim said, was the biggest development of all. 'The first thing Billie said she loved about Ritchie was the fact that he didn't drink. She would have a glass of red wine and that would last the whole evening. She would just sip at it. She was always frightened that if she did get drunk, it would get back to her mum, Mandy. But there is a harder edge to Billie now. She has changed so much.'

Each of these three worried adults were desperately hoping that Billie could turn off what they saw as a dangerously wrong road in her life. They genuinely wanted to guide her back to what they felt was a safer world and, every time they spoke of Billie, they hoped she might somehow hear and learn from their words.

Other people were far less honourable in their intentions, however. Many so-called friends were happy to offer their 'advice' to Billie via the generous conduits of tabloid newspaper reporters. Others who had no real connection with her at all were happy for a moment in the spotlight as they pontificated on her situation. And, worst of all, was the growing sense in the media that

Billie's latest script had already been written — a sense that everyone was willing her to play her part in yet another tale of crash-and-burn celebrity. The idea was that Billie's career — and her life — had gone into some sort of freefall and that meeting Chris had accelerated her decline. One of the more ridiculous arguments raised against her was that her time as a teenage star meant she was pre-programmed to agree with whatever any older man told her to say or do.

Away from the cameras, the truth about Billie and Chris's relationship was very different, of course. What the reporters didn't know, or didn't want to report, was a far more disturbing story starting to unfold in a far less exciting part of London. For all the headlines about drunken evenings and hungover mornings, the early months of Billie's relationship with Chris hadn't all been about parties, pubs and pints in the West End. Behind the scenes, Billie, Chris and her parents were all being forced to face up to the very real pressures of life in the public eye. The support Chris was offering Billie would underpin their relationship and give it a strength few people had ever anticipated.

Billie's new ordeal would come in an anonymous central London courtroom where she would finally come face to face with the woman who had repeatedly threatened to kill her. The worst month of her life was about to begin... and Chris would be by her side for every day of it.

6
DEATH THREATS

'BILLIE PIPER'S HEAD needs cutting off… she needs decapitating and killing. She needs her body set on fire and her body burnt to cinders.'

This was just one of the chilling death threats that Billie had been forced to listen to, aged just 17, when she was called into her record company offices in late August 2000. Other threats, all delivered during an extraordinary 11-day hate campaign, were equally savage. The same caller repeatedly attacked Billie as a 'whore' and a 'cow', and threatened her with dismemberment, burning, flogging and shooting. Even her family weren't safe from the threats. 'Billie Piper is a bloody pig and I am going to kill her parents,' ran one of the messages. 'I see them out shopping all the time. They're going to get their heads cut off very soon. The silly cow is a silly bitch. She can sing and dance but she's a bitch. She is going to be dead.'

Other messages told Mandy and Paul to be ready for 'a bullet through the head' while Billie's young brother Charlie was also feared to be a target. One of the other 13 hate-filled messages seemed to mention his name and ended with a peal of maniacal laughter. And there were, of course, ever more threats to Billie herself — including the most chilling of all: 'Next time she appears on stage, she is going to be shot dead.'

It was little more than a year since the BBC's *Crimewatch* presenter Jill Dando had been killed on the doorstep of her west London home. Fears over deranged stalkers were still running high and a blonde teenage pop star like Billie Piper was seen as a desperately vulnerable target, especially one who had been attracting a mix of hate mail and obscene correspondence since her earliest days in the public eye.

When Billie had made her first record, her parents had set up and run a fan club from the family home in Swindon. A huge number of fans seemed to write in, often simply addressing the letters to: 'Billie Piper, Pop Star, Swindon.' At that point, Mandy and Paul were happy to send out photographs and even personal replies to some of the nicest letters. But over the months, they say two things then changed. First, as Billie's career became even more successful, the sheer volume of mail meant they were no longer able to cope with the job from home. Then, as news broke that she was dating Ritchie Neville, the tone and content of the letters deteriorated rapidly. His fans bombarded Billie's fan club

Young Billie worked hard growing the grass-roots of her pop career. Seen here on *The Big Breakfast*, Power in the Park, a Radio 1 Roadshow and on *CD:UK*, all in 1998.

Above: Sylvia Young, the woman who nurtured Billie's burgeoning acting and showbiz talent.

Below left: Nicki Chapman, *Popstars* and *Pop Idol* judge and Billie's agent.

Below right: In the early days, Billie found support in Martine McCutcheon, seen here at the Capital Radio Awards in 2000.

Above: Billie shows off her breakthrough No. 1 single, 'Because We Want To', released from her debut album *Honey to the B*.

Below left: Billie performing live at the *Smash Hits* Awards, Cardiff, in December 1998.

Below right: Brunette Billie turns up the heat in red at the 1999 Brit Awards, though she went home empty-handed.

Above left: Partying in the Park – Hyde Park, London, July 2000.

Above right: Promoting 'Day & Night', the lead single from her second album, *Walk of Life*.

Below: Filming the video for the Number 1 hit 'Day & Night', May 2000.

Above left: Billie arrives for the party to mark the launch of her new album *Walk of Life* at Papa Gaio in London's West End.

Above right: Billie celebrates turning 18. Her dad Paul is in the background.

Below left: More than a touch of the Britney style as Billie performs at the *Smash Hits* Poll Winners' Party held at the London Arena in December 2000.

Below right: Doing her bit on stage in Dublin for the charity Childline in January 2001.

Billie's first high-profile love was 5ive boy-band member, Ritchie Neville (below, centre). The couple were close before drifting apart under pressure of their hectic careers.

Above left: Billie beams with happiness as she weds radio DJ, TV presenter and media star Chris Evans in a quickie ceremony in Las Vegas.

Above right: Fresh out of the chapel, the couple stroll away, followed by a handful of close friends.

Below left: Mr and Mrs Evans take a shopping stroll round Palm Springs, California on their honeymoon.

Below right: On their way to their local in west London.

Billie became the focus of media commentators everywhere as she and Chris were often spotted out drinking. Here the newlyweds enjoy yet another celebratory tipple.

with aggressive and unpleasant comments, drawings and worse. Desperate to shield their daughter from the way a minority of people seemed to perceive her, and sickened by what they were now forced to read on a daily basis, Mandy and Paul passed the job of running the fan club over to the professionals at Innocent Records. Any post still sent to their house in Swindon was forwarded, unopened, to London. And the Post Office was told that this was now the proper destination for all the vaguely addressed mail that was still being sent to Billie almost every day.

Unfortunately, some letters would always go astray or fail to get a reply. And as the jury at Blackfriars Crown Court would soon find out, one particular unanswered letter was to help trigger one of the most virulent hate campaigns music executives could remember. The industry's view is that most of the unpleasant letters sent to celebrities are horrible, but harmless. The events which would unfold for Billie were something else altogether.

It had all begun in May 2000 when music fan Juliet Peters and a friend had got free tickets to the filming of the *Pepsi Chart Show* on Channel Five. Billie had been the week's guest presenter and Juliet had managed to stand close to her when Billie read a few words from the autocue just before one of the commercial breaks. Under ordinary circumstances, that would have been that. But when the show was broadcast, on 11 May, a friend said it appeared as if Billie was looking directly at Juliet when she started speaking. Juliet hadn't liked it at all. When the matter came to court, she admitted she had brooded about the supposedly disrespectful glance for several days before writing to Billie's fan club to complain about it. 'Why did you give me such a sly, dirty look out of the corner of your eyes before you introduced the break? Who do you think you are, you prima donna?' she wrote in a letter she signed 'Yours angrily'.

No one is clear whether the letter was ever spotted amidst all the other mail Billie was receiving at this point. And as so many of the other letters contained even worse comments from Ritchie Neville fans, it certainly didn't attract any attention or seem to merit a reply. With hindsight, this was a big mistake.

Back at her home in Canning Town, east London, Juliet admits she continued to let her anger fester and finally snapped on the evening of 14 August 2000. She tracked down the phone number for Innocent Records and rang to leave her first message for Billie at 3.09am. Four more calls that evening would be timed at 3.11am, 3.13am, 3.21am and 3.47am, and they would provide a series of shocks for the record company staff who checked the machine as normal when they arrived in the office the following morning.

After replaying them several times, the Innocent executives decided the level of the threats was so high that they needed to let Billie, her family and the police know what was going on. This did not seem to be something which could be dismissed as just another rant from a disaffected fan. When it comes to criticism, pop music bosses have normally heard it all before, but these messages were clearly in a different league.

Billie was on her way back from yet another promotional tour, this time to Canada, and she was asked to go to Innocent's offices to listen to the tapes almost as soon as she cleared Customs. By this time, the police were ready to take up the case and were waiting to talk to the teenager about the threats. First, though, the jet-lagged and vulnerable Billie had to hear the messages for herself.

'They were just horrific,' she told the court afterwards when the caller had been identified and sent to trial. 'I could not understand why anyone would want to say these things. I had done nothing personal and had no intention of upsetting anyone and it just seemed very bizarre and made me cry. I don't think anyone should have to listen to that. I could only listen to the first two and I began to listen to the third and they were just awful. They were the worst things I ever had to listen to.'

Unfortunately for them, the record company's workers were to hear many more of the threats in the coming days. The office answering machine would be flickering with yet more ugly messages for the next 11 mornings before the caller was apprehended. Even then, life could not go back to normal for Billie. The police told her they wanted to prosecute the caller – not least to deter others from thinking such venomous activities could ever go unpunished.

So, on 5 February 2001, Juliet was taken to court for

making five threats against Billie and four against her parents. A very public trial was to take place, putting even more pressure on the whole Piper family. 'It really doesn't matter whether you have performed on stage in front of thousands in a theatre or in a concert. Nothing can really prepare you for taking the stand in a courtroom,' says Barrister Neil Godfrey. 'It is nerve-wracking for anyone, at any age. However much the court staff try to put you at your ease, there is a silence and a formality to court proceedings which takes years to get used to. The other shock if you are giving evidence against someone is the fact that they are likely to be sitting just a few feet away from you. They are likely to be staring at you as you speak about them and about what they have done. Ninety-nine times out of a hundred, it will not be a pleasant experience.'

For Billie, the stress of her 20-minute spell in the witness box was made worse by the tone of the questions she was asked under oath. Each of the chilling messages had been played to the court before Juliet's barrister, Tom MacKinnon asked, 'Is this not just the downside of being a pop star?'

'I am not criticising you, Miss Piper,' the barrister continued. 'But it's correct, isn't it, that despite these unpleasant, wild death threats and a woman threatening to bury an axe in your head, nothing happened in terms of being attacked?' The barrister also pointed to the poison-pen letters Billie had received at her fan club the previous year when she had started dating Ritchie

Neville – letters Billie said were in a quite different league to the telephone threats over the incident at the *Pepsi Chart Show*.

'They were all very scary but, because they were written, I did not really think that much about it,' Billie said. 'The guy I was going out with was a heart-throb and a lot of fans who were jealous or did not like me believed that he was their boyfriend and they were going to marry him.'

When she was in the witness box, Billie's mother agreed, telling the court there was 'no comparison' between the silly threats in letters from teenagers and the verbal threats from a grown woman with an irrational grudge.

As the case continued, Billie's dad Paul also took to the stand and at issue during his evidence was the message which referred to 'Charlie'. Peters said this was simply a reference to cocaine and the allegations that Billie took drugs. But Paul said it had been impossible for the whole family not to think it was a direct threat to their young son. 'He is just a little boy. He wants to play in the street and I've got to watch him all the time making sure no one is stalking him,' Paul told the court.

As the barristers summed up the evidence for the jury, there were further, chilling reminders of the potential seriousness of Billie's situation. 'It is a fact that, sadly, people in the public eye can and do attract dangerous and unwanted attention and deserve protection,' said prosecutor Mark Aldred. He specifically mentioned former Beatle John Lennon, shot dead by fan Mark Chapman in 1980 and George Harrison who, more recently, had been stabbed by a fan in his Oxfordshire home. Most people, though, were more likely to be still thinking of Jill Dando's fate a year earlier — something Billie herself had had in her mind since the taped threats had first been played to her.

After the trial ended, Juliet was found guilty of threatening behaviour and a series of other charges and, in a rare move, the foreman of the jury, comprising seven women and five men, passed the judge a note they had written asking that she be given psychiatric help with her problems.

Billie, who had attended almost every day of the trial with Chris and her parents, decided not to return to Blackfriars Crown Court when Juliet was sentenced on 2 March 2001. And in many ways that was just as well. Judge Brian Pryor QC had strong words but no custodial sentence for Billie's former fan. 'It may be that you did not fully appreciate the pain and fear to the Piper family that your actions caused,' he said. 'But you knew what you were doing was wrong, you were obviously out to upset them and, of course, you did.' He said the language in Peters' threats had been 'bizarre, obscene and savage', all of which made them even more powerful. 'It gave a picture of intense hatred and great determination which must have made the people listening more fearful than they may have been if they had been threats from some young teenagers,' he concluded.

But Juliet did still get to walk free from the court. She was handed out an 18-month suspended jail sentence and a two-year supervision order. Outside the court, Detective Constable Victoria Merron praised Billie's decision to give evidence during the trial, saying it would act as a deterrent against other stalkers and should protect other people in the public eye from harassment. Billie, though, rightly refused to comment any more on the case. It had been a terrible time for her, reinforcing all her growing disillusionment with the music industry. But now it was over she simply wanted to move on. The only thing she did want to say was 'thank you' to her supporters – the fans who had sent positive messages and those closer to home who had been with her every day in court.

Chris Evans – the man whom the newspaper columnists said was likely to ruin her life and drag her down with booze and bad behaviour – had, instead, been her 'rock' in the dark days of the trial. 'I don't think I could have gone through the court case without his support and that of my parents,' she said after the verdict had been given and the sentencing had been handed down. 'This week has not been great. It has been bad, but it has been dealt with now. I said my piece in court. It was a shock to the system but it is over now.'

With this terrible chapter in her life closed Billie struggled to carry on with her public life as normal. She kept her long-standing commitments to the year's Comic Relief effort with a football-themed photo-call in Central London, for example. And she spent a day filming a promotional video for the World Vision charity that was hoping to raise new funds for its educational work with children in the developing world.

Despite all this activity, several people who knew Billie well noticed subtle and worrying changes in her manner and lifestyle. 'At the beginning of her career, Billie was confident and uncomplicatedly enthusiastic about the joys of shooting to Number One at the age of 15,' says *Telegraph* writer Cassandra Jardine, who met Billie many times over her career and had followed all the recent reports of her supposed party lifestyle. In 2001, Cassandra saw very little evidence of any new lightness of mood. 'In those early days, Billie would conduct interviews on her own and was touchingly confiding. But things have changed. Too much has happened to her career, her health and her love life since then for this pop princess to trust others' goodwill any more.' So after Peters had been freed from court, Billie was accompanied by two minders for her next *Telegraph* profile and photo-shoot. Her world, somehow, had got smaller and more than ever she was looking for a way to escape it.

At the end of March, it was back to the office for Billie, though not quite back to work. The team that had worked with her at Innocent had shrunk since the start of the year, and the relative failure of 'Walk of Life'. Her spokesperson, Vital Publicity's Dave Pittman, was no longer representing her and, after the split, had told the media, 'As far as I know, all further enquiries will be forwarded on to her record company, Virgin. We feel we got as far as we could go with Billie.'

Hot on the heels of that change, Billie also parted company with her long-term manager and agent Nicki Chapman – though not in the acrimonious terms which were described in the papers. The truth was that after a professional partnership lasting nearly three years, both sides were ready for a change. And after finding huge new fame on *Popstars* and *Pop Idol*, Nicki was keen to rationalise her other activities. She had just been made creative director of impresario Simon Fuller's 19 Entertainment and signed a lucrative presenting contract with the BBC. With Billie growing up fast and being able to handle more of her own affairs, it seemed a natural time for Nicki to bow out.

Perhaps one of the reasons for all the stories saying Billie had been sacked by Nicki (or the other way around, depending on your choice of paper) was that both sides refused to say anything about the change, and the papers simply found whatever rumour they could to fill the vacuum. Only after the stories seemed to get out of control did the pair agree that Nicki should speak. Her message was clear: 'When I stopped working with Billie, I always said I wouldn't discuss her publicly, as when you manage someone there is always an element of trust. We are still friends, and I want it to stay that way. If I do an interview, however glowing, the papers will then expect me to comment on her each time something happens in her life.'

Sitting at the boardroom table at Innocent, the grown-up Billie was ready to prove that she could look after herself. Everyone had decided that Billie's re-working of Blondie's 'The Tide Is High' should be her next single — even though Billie herself had taken some persuading to release a cover rather than a new song. Where she did want to put her foot down, however, was over the release date. It's feel-good stuff, it's a summer song, she argued; putting it out in the spring seemed like a mistake and would almost certainly guarantee her two badly-performing singles in a row. She won her argument and, in the process, bought herself a bit of time.

What she wanted to do with this extra time was simple; she wanted to switch off from the rest of the world, spend time with Chris and catch up on being herself. Chris, whose Virgin Radio contract gave him 12 weeks' holiday a year (as well as his multi-million pound salary), was more than ready to help. After their mini-break in Madeira, they soon headed to Spain for some late winter sunshine at the £340-a-night, five-star Byblos hotel on the Costa del Sol, where fellow guests (who were pounced upon by British reporters whenever they left the hotel grounds) said they seemed totally in love and very happy together. The hotel promises a state-of-the-art health spa for guests in need of total relaxation. Billie and Chris happily made the most of it.

Just before April Fool's Day (which is also Chris's birthday), Billie and Chris nipped over to Paris for a romantic couple of days walking along the Seine, eating great food and drinking in the classic smoke-filled bars of the Left Bank. By now, Billie felt extraordinarily relaxed in Chris's company – and extraordinarily happy with the way her life had suddenly turned out. She and Chris were still able to talk the day and the night away about anything and everything. They still laughed, seemingly endlessly, over the smallest of things – the people around them, the things they saw, the things they had been through. And they seemed to support each other. With Chris at her side, Billie felt she had a bubble of protection from all the stresses and problems of her life in the public eye. Album sales, the singles charts, the pop programmes and the promotional schedule all seemed a million miles away. For the first time since leaving Bradon Forest Comprehensive and enrolling in the hot-house atmosphere of Sylvia Young's, Billie felt free. She no longer felt on a treadmill of classes, performance and perfection. She no longer felt she needed to please everyone from the youngest fan to the most powerful executive at her record company. If someone said "Jump", she would no longer have to ask "How high?" – or what she should wear when she did. Being a pop star might have bought her financial freedom, but it had imprisoned her in a persona and a schedule that she had been desperate to escape.

Chris's attitude to her situation was clean and simple; he simply shrugged and told her that if she wanted a break, she should take one. He said her life was more important than her career, her happiness more valuable than another

Number One. And Billie knew he was right; she had made enough money, and broken enough records. It is a cliché to say that sometimes you want a single moment to last for ever, but as Billie looked out over the lights of Paris that spring, she felt just that about the calmness, the safety and the security she felt with Chris. And so, hardly believing what she was doing, she said something extraordinary… she asked Chris to marry her.

It was, she admits, a throw-away line, the kind of comment you make in passing, as a joke, and without expecting to be taken seriously. And far from eliciting a serious response, Billie's question instead triggered a lengthy debate about whether or not it was a leap year (it wasn't). By the time they had ended this discussion, the original question had been pushed a little bit into the background – which seemed the best place for it. But both knew that the genie was now out of the bottle. If one person in a relationship raises the question of marriage, and the other one doesn't run for the hills, then a clear message about the future has been sent. Without saying a word, Billie stored away the fact that Chris hadn't run anywhere.

7
WEDDING BELLS

BACK IN BRITAIN, the rumour mill had picked up on the idea that a Paris proposal might have taken place — although it missed the fact that it had been Billie, rather than Chris, who had popped the question. So one morning in April, the media scrum was back outside the Belgravia flat where Chris and Billie stayed in London, to find out if wedding bells really were in the air. And Chris and Billie decided to escape the questions by getting on another plane.

At Easter, they headed to Portugal where they joined some of Chris's golfing pals and checked in to the ritzy £260-a-night Dona Felipa hotel in the Vale do Lobo. In theory, a hotel set in its own extensive grounds would offer plenty of privacy to the likes of Billie and Chris. In reality, tabloid newspapers simply booked their reporters into as many of its rooms as they could find and started the cameras clicking.

The papers' plan was to illustrate as many stories as possible of Billie and Chris celebrating what was still a totally unconfirmed engagement – hopes were high that the pair might throw a wild party and misbehave as the wine started to flow. But, in fact, Billie and Chris hadn't made any serious plans about the future. So what the reporters and photographers saw instead was the perfect picture of a couple entirely happy doing what they wanted, when they wanted. Chris and his two friends played golf every day, while Chris wore the same shirt and shorts for the whole trip, triggering endless comment in the papers about his unromantic nature. Billie, meanwhile, wanted to be as calm and relaxed as possible. She spent her days in glorious solitude, lying by the pool reading magazines and smoking. When Chris came back from the course, he would ruffle Billie's hair and softly kiss the top of her head. She spread a little suntan cream on the back of his neck and they chatted quietly in their self-protecting bubble. These were quiet moments of genuine affection, part of an increasingly comfortable and secure relationship.

The subject of marriage had not been raised since Paris, but Billie knew she wanted Chris in her life for the long term. So many people had already said he was a bad influence on her; many more would say so in the months and years ahead. But she knew that he calmed her down like no one had ever done before. Sitting alongside him in the Portuguese sunshine, she felt serene, confident and strong.

When she had first hit Number One with 'Because We Want To' in 1998, she had said that had been the best year of her life. With less than four months gone and, despite a terrible court case, she felt 2001 had easily surpassed it. And she had high hopes for every day of the rest of it.

Wedding bells were very much in the air when Billie and Chris left Portugal and headed back to Hascombe Court, the Surrey home that Billie had first visited on Christmas Day. The property is one of the most stunning in the county, looking like the backdrop to every period drama that has ever been filmed. It had been built in 1908 by a pupil of celebrated architect Sir Edwin Lutyens and, as well as the vast estate, has a formal garden designed by the equally top-notch horticulturalist Gertrude Jeckyll. Chris had already done a huge amount of work refurbishing and restoring the interior (acquiring a Grade II listing from English Heritage in the process), and had easily won over locals who had feared that a DJ would be neither a responsible property owner or a decent neighbour. With Billie living there pretty much full-time when they weren't abroad or in London, there were high hopes that the house might soon be the site of the biggest celebrity wedding of the year.

If they did tie the knot in such a wonderful setting then publicity experts said they could easily sell the photographic rights for a then British record of more than £1 million – though Chris and Billie both said that, if this ever happened, they would break celebrity convention and donate the full proceeds to charity. But was there really going to be a wedding? Neither Billie nor Chris would confirm or deny the rumours — not least because they were still so relaxed about the subject that they had barely discussed it themselves. But Billie didn't exactly dampen the mood when she was seen looking at wedding dresses in Harrods one lazy afternoon — fellow shoppers said she had set her heart on a traditional white gown costing a relatively modest £3,000.

Another month, another plane trip — and this was going to be the big one. In May, Billie and Chris flew to California, the first time Billie had been in the States since the crisis of confidence at her Chicago concert the previous year. This time, though, she was blissfully happy to be on the other side of the Atlantic. First stop was Los Angeles, where the weather was unusually cold and dark. The Hollywood sign was wet with rain and the smog was building up as the clouds refused to lift. So Billie and Chris headed east, to the desert town of Palm Springs, the former 'playground of the stars', where the likes of Frank Sinatra, Elvis Presley, Liberace and Cary Grant all bought homes in the golden age of Hollywood.

Today, Palm Springs is trying to reclaim its former glory, promoting its modernist desert homes as architectural jewels and its vast green golf courses as environmental wonders. There is still a small, calm and almost frontier town feel about the place and it was there, in the shadow of the vast San Jacinto mountain range, that Billie realised just how happy she was with

Chris. The fact that they were in America at all, let alone
the way they were darting around it to chase the sun,
was all due to Chris's typically reckless, impulsive and
unpredictable moods. This inability to sit still could
drive some people mad, but for Billie it was an
inspiration, proof that life didn't always have to be lived
at the dictates of a record company, a PR adviser or a
promotions executive.

For his part, Chris was still over the moon at being
with someone who had the guts to treat life as one big
adventure. He loved the fact that Billie was suddenly so
open to new experiences and ready to treat every day as
if it could be her last. It seemed as if the couple really
were soulmates and that no one else could ever be as well
suited. So it seemed as if it really was time to get married
and prove to the world that this was more than some
media stunt or passing phase.

The next day, Billie and Chris decided to go for it – in
style. The big MGM production of a wedding in
Hascombe Court was never going to happen. Instead, they
felt like superstars, flying into Nevada in a tiny private
plane. They had decided to get married in Las Vegas.

Harrah's Casino Hotel on the Las Vegas strip was both
a surprising and a very typical choice for the couple. It
was surprising because it is far from the ritziest or most
exclusive of the Las Vegas mega-hotels. If they had wanted
opulence, glamour and six-star service they could have
gone to Bellagio, the Venetian or even Caesar's Palace.
Harrah's, meanwhile, reflected the more old-fashioned,

down-to-earth Vegas of a slightly earlier age. And it was this that made it the perfect choice for Billie and Chris who wanted an authentic Vegas experience with some rat-pack glamour thrown in for free.

And it wasn't as if they were slumming it — out of the 2,500 Harrah's rooms on offer they had one of the nicest £175-a-night suites from which to plot their big day. Four of Chris's closest friends had been told of the couple's plans and had jumped on planes to witness it. Danny Baker was first to arrive — and as he had already been on two holidays with Billie and Chris, it felt like old times to welcome him to this latest adventure. The other arrivals were Virgin Radio producer Chris Gillett, his girlfriend Zara and the station's sports newsreader John Webster — Webbo to Chris, Billie and his fans.

The notable absentees where Billie's parents and Chris's mother. Deciding not to have family at their ceremony had been a wrench for Billie, in particular. She knew her mother would be furious at missing out (and was proved right as the pair fell out over it and barely spoke for some time afterwards). But two factors made Billie carry on regardless. First, she had been worried that if they had turned up, Mandy and Paul would have tried to persuade their daughter to slow down and marry in a more traditional manner at some point in the future. Secondly, Billie had been worried that the press would have found out if she had made the call and had her whole family fly out of Heathrow. All she wanted to do, she said, was to marry Chris and become husband and wife. Neither of them wanted to star in a media circus. So with a heavy heart, Billie prepared to get married the way she had prepared for almost all of the challenges she had faced in her life so far – on her own.

As wedding days go, Billie's was typically off the wall from the start. Early in the day, she and Chris decided they might want to wear something new for the ceremony – so they headed to the far from glitzy Banana Republic in the shopping mall across the strip from their hotel. Then they realised they were hungry, so they had a huge Vegas steak with all the trimmings by the pool back at Harrah's. Then, in the early evening, they went back to their suite, had a new discussion about what to wear and headed off to their church. And it wasn't just any church. Billie and Chris had booked their service at the Little Church of the West at the southern end of the Las Vegas strip.

The Little Church was built in 1942, making it the oldest structure still standing on the city's main street. It is built out of cedar and redwood, is designed to look like a miniature version of an Old West mining town church, and is the American equivalent of a listed building. And despite being an easy target for mockery, the church is nowhere near as tacky as many people imagine. It sells itself as being 'an oasis of love and romance' and sits in its own one-acre plot of surprisingly green gardens at a decent distance from the neon and noise of the major hotels further up the street. Billie and Chris also loved the fact that they had both seen the church in the classic 1964 Elvis Presley film *Viva Las Vegas*.

A limousine took the couple down past the mock skyscrapers of the New York New York hotel, past the vast black glass pyramid of Luxor and drew up in the church grounds, just opposite Robbie Williams' favourite Vegas haunt, Mandalay Bay. Their ceremony had cost them just $250 dollars, and was the second-most expensive of the four packages on offer at the chapel. This bought them the five-minute ceremony, a single buttonhole for the groom, a small bouquet of teardrop roses that Billie carried as she walked down the aisle, an organist, a set of glossy photographs and a video of the event.

But before it began, the pair had to wait to get their actual marriage licence and Billie, the 18-year-old who had lived most of her life in a hurry, was for once happy with the delay. 'I hate queuing so much but this was the happiest queue in the world. It's all women in dresses about to go off to the church. It's just so brilliant,' she said. Several of these women were dressed up to the nines, as they would have done if they had been at any other wedding. But Billie had no big white meringue of a dress. Instead, she was just wearing a midriff-revealing white shirt knotted at the waist, a long pink sarong and flip flops. Chris was wearing an open-necked, pale-blue shirt, beige striped trousers and sunglasses.

Wagner's *Lohengrin* and 'All I Ask of You' from *The Phantom of the Opera* were playing on the organ as the couple headed down and back up the aisle – faces beaming with excitement and Billie's smile as wide as it has ever been. Danny Baker had the video running, just in case the in-house version from the chapel didn't work out. In less than ten minutes, Billie Piper and Chris Evans were husband and wife.

'It was the standard service, with some vows, a bit of scripture and a prayer which runs to five minutes in the spoken part,' said Chapel manager Greg Smith. 'There were some tears and then they kissed, a lovely kiss, and everyone applauded.' Greg said the one difference between Billie and Chris's wedding and the many others he oversees was the fact that Billie and Chris didn't exchange rings. Chris doesn't like jewellery and Billie was too pleased to be married to care about details. On reflection, even missing out on rings wasn't as unusual as it might seem for Vegas brides. 'When Richard Gere married Cindy Crawford here, they made their own rings out of foil chewing-gum wrappers, but Billie and Chris were happy to do it without rings altogether,' said Greg. He was also pleased that the couple did manage to keep their ceremony private. 'Billie is a striking girl but no one really recognised her because she is not a pop star over in America – though I recognised him from the English men's magazines,' he said, having handed over the paperwork and waved the newlyweds goodbye.

Smiling even more broadly, the couple picked up the free bottle of champagne on offer from the chapel and both swigged from it as they headed out on the town.

Billie, who strictly speaking was too young to be in the casinos, let alone to gamble big money there, was giggling and laughing while her new husband twirled her around in the air on the way back to their hotel suite and promised to try carrying her over the thresholds when they got back to their many homes in Britain. They then did a mini-tour of some of the main casinos with the rest of the small wedding party. And to this day, Billie gets furious with people who say there was anything wrong or tacky about her unique big day.

'Chris and I were like excited kids. It was our day and nothing else mattered. The whole thing was just great… it was really romantic. And it was so typical of him and of me. It was full of personality and that is what any marriage should be.'

Billie also showed she had far more traditional views about love and marriage than their Vegas adventure suggested. As far as she was concerned, this was the real thing. The location and the method of their marriage were irrelevant. What mattered to her was its message. 'We did it because it is too temporary otherwise. It is too easy to walk out on something if you are not married,' she said. And she didn't want to walk out on Chris, or have him walk out on her. Both felt they had found total happiness in each other and they wanted to do everything they could to protect it.

'We are delighted to formally announce that Chris Evans and Billie Piper have married. We wish Chris and Billie every happiness and look forward to celebrating with them when Chris returns to the breakfast show next Monday.' The public confirmation of what had become a widely leaked marriage was given by Virgin Radio DJ Nick Abbot on the following day's drive-time show. But would the marriage last? As the public digested the news, it was pointed out that the odds looked stacked against them – and not just because of the age gap between Billie and Chris and the short amount of time that they had been dating. The problem lay with the Little Church of the West itself. It prides itself as being 'the scene of more celebrity marriages than any other chapel on earth'. But quantity does not always mean quality and the track record of its most famous clients hardly inspires much confidence.

Vegas and film historians say the rot set in early. Betty Grable and Harry James were pretty much the first celebrity couple to marry there in 1943, with Zsa Zsa Gabor and George Sanders, Judy Garland and Mickey Rooney following suit over the next few years. After filming there in 1964, Elvis Presley was back for real in 1967 when he married Priscilla, while more recent couples include Bruce Willis and Demi Moore, Richard Gere and Cindy Crawford, Bob Geldof and Paula Yates, Noel Gallagher and Meg Matthews, Dennis Rodman and Carmen Electra. It doesn't take a *Mastermind* champion to spot the common denominator of most of those big-name couples – the fact that precious few of them subsequently escaped the divorce court.

'There's no guarantee of eternal happiness,' admits the

chapel's resident Elvis impersonator Ron DeCar, who serenades newlyweds and sang at Noel and Meg's wedding. But Billie and Chris were certainly hoping to be the exception that proves the rule. And back in Britain, after a couple more days' honeymooning back in Palm Springs, their first challenge was to appease their respective parents. In Swindon, Mandy and Paul were the biggest hurdle, taking some time to come to terms with this latest evidence of how fast their highly ambitious daughter had grown up.

What made matters worse was the continuous drip, drip, drip of criticism of the couple. Billie's vain hope after tying the knot was that this would stop the critics in their tracks. By proving she and Chris were serious about each other and had entered into an adult, lifetime commitment, she hoped they would be left alone. She hoped in vain — and much of the new wave of attacks were even more ferocious than they had been in the past. Others were hilariously over the top. The *Daily Mirror*'s famed royal reporter James Whittaker was one of the first to make his feelings known — and in no uncertain terms. 'What on earth are Chris Evans and Billie Piper up to?' he asked in his weekly column. 'Dreadful that it should be so, but these two are icons to the young. It is bad enough what this talented man is doing job-wise, but his marriage is being conducted, often publicly, in the most appalling manner. Lasciviousness, drunkenness, yobbish behaviour and a complete lack of respect by the ghastly Evans to his child bride sets a terrible example and upsets the horses. The whole institution of matrimony is being mocked. How come they were allowed to marry? I suppose they went about it in secret to stop sane people being involved.'

In other coverage, Billie was damned as 'a pop star of tender years and an uncertain future,' while Chris was all but accused of brainwashing her. 'As in all age–gap marriages, the young ingénue gets a teacher/lover/father–figure all rolled up into one, while the older husband gets the chance to be the boss,' was one unkind interpretation of the Evans dynamic.

Wedding magazine writer Francesca Bell said this kind of criticism was particularly hurtful at a time when Billie should have been euphoric. 'Every wedding magazine I have ever worked on has surveyed new brides and found they fall into two distinct categories. Those who have spent months if not years planning very big, elaborate weddings are often exhausted and deflated in the aftermath. But those who marry quickly without any planning or stress tend to be on a high after the event. They get the fun of telling people, surprising people and defying expectations. The constant belittling aimed at Billie on her return from Las Vegas was cruel. She hadn't done anything wrong, but she could be excused for somehow assuming that she had.'

Billie's reaction to the criticism was to go into retreat. She and Chris spent even more time together, gradually excluding others from their joint lives. They continued to split their time between London and Surrey and –

most importantly – they continued to be happy together.

Having desperately needed Chris's support when she was giving evidence in her 'hate message' court case earlier in the year, Billie was ready to return the favour for her new husband in slightly less extreme circumstances. He was called to Staines Magistrates' Court after being clocked driving at 105mph on the A3. Interestingly enough, Billie, who had worn all green to give evidence in her own case was wearing all black on the day she went to support her husband. They walked into the suburban building hand-in-hand, waving discreetly at a few bystanders before Chris was fined £600 with £35 costs and banned for 56 days. It was yet more encouragement for Billie to learn to drive herself, though one more reason why she wanted to steer clear of the super-fast Ferrari that had made her fall in love with Chris less than six months ago.

Billie's whole look changed even more in the couple's first summer together. The perfectly groomed young pop star had already given way to a more grungily dressed alternative. Now she started washing her hair just once a week and said she loved the matted bird's nest that it became. 'Sometimes, Chris says it is like waking up with Rod Stewart because my hair is so busy and big in the morning. My ambition is never to brush my hair again.'

The rest of Billie's look was treated in a similar manner. 'I am going through a bit of a rebellious stage because, ever since I left school, I was preened and groomed, but maybe I am not designed to be stick-thin and wear tiny skirts and platform shoes,' she said. 'I hate shaving my legs and plucking my eyebrows. I don't care about all that shit. I have gym wear, sleep wear and going to the shops wear and sometimes I can be in the same stuff for days at a time.'

Chris thought it was all hilarious. When he wasn't calling Billie by his new nickname of 'Wifey', he was holding her hand and calling her 'my pretty little scruff'. He and Billie would sometimes drive into town in matching Hawaiian shirts for a laugh and Chris told his friends that the more relaxed Billie became about her appearance the more he loved her.

Billie's mum Mandy could hardly have missed the transformation but, after recovering from the shock of the wedding, she was totally supportive of her eldest daughter. 'Yes, she and Chris seem to have turned into a scruffier version of Posh and Becks,' Mandy admitted with a laugh. 'Billie used to get very upset when there were pictures of her in the paper making her look fat or a mess. But the other day, there was a picture of her popping out wearing an old tracksuit and she couldn't care less. I am just happy because Billie is happy. Since the wedding, she seems so much more settled. She is under less pressure and finally able to sit back and look at things in perspective.'

At the end of the day, Mandy and Paul were aware that their daughter had to grow up and grow even further away some time. And they said they were simply glad that she was finally free to live (and dress) as she wanted, rather than being forced to conform to the rules set down by the homogenous pop world. Slowly but surely, a few other people started to take on the same view. The more Billie ignored the critics, the stronger she clearly was. And this alone seemed worthy of respect. She and Chris started to be seen as the biggest breath of fresh air in showbusiness, a couple who were prepared to throw convention to the wind, ignore the PR spinners and just get on with having fun.

'They were a hilarious antidote to the tedious celebrity trend of "power coupling". There were no matching outfits on the red carpet for Billie and Chris. It was just, "I'll have what you're having and sod it if it costs me my liver and my career,"' was how *Arena* writer Steve Beale saw it. The actor Danny Dyer, whom Billie had been dating casually just before meeting Chris, was one of the few to try and get the message across that Billie was happy. 'When I speak to her on the phone, she always says, "I'm so loved up, Dan, this is fantastic." When she rang me out of the blue to say she was married, she was over the moon. The age gap between her and Chris is massive but she's not worried about that and she's not an idiot. She says she has never been so happy in her life.'

Danny, fresh from his success on *Human Traffic* and Mel Smith's *High Heels and Low Lifes*, also proved himself to be a gentleman by defending his former girlfriend on other fronts as well. He said that the Billie he had known had proved she had the inner steel to cope with anything life threw at her. 'All the stuff about her collapsing in nightclubs because of drugs was rubbish. She collapsed because of exhaustion She was very young, only 17, when I was seeing her. But she was never immature. She's level-headed, clued up and strong.'

Billie, meanwhile, was simply loving her new-found freedom. 'It was absolutely wonderful to be able to leave the house looking like absolute shit and just not to care,' says Billie. 'That was something I had never been allowed to do as a pop star. And I had been a pop star since I was 15 so I'd had my fill of it.' On a personal level, she said Chris boosted her confidence by proving he loved the woman inside of her, not just the image she sent out to the world. 'With other people I had been out with, I had worried about how I looked and all that, but with Chris I didn't care because I knew he didn't care about it. That made me feel so much better.'

At their big kitchen in Hascombe Court, Chris said he was trying to teach his previously undomestic goddess of a wife how to cook. But what everyone else seemed to see was that he was continuing to teach her to drink. The pair were firmly entrenched as regulars at the White Horse pub in the village near to their house. They became great friends with the landlord James Ward and his business partner Susan Barnett and were thrilled to be so accepted into the heart of village life. When they weren't drinking there – where a typically scruffy Billie was infamously photographed one day simultaneously holding a mobile phone, a cigarette and a pint – they were at The Nag's Head or The Grenadier in

Knightsbridge or any of the crowded bars around the Groucho Club in Soho. One paper even carried out a regular 'booze audit' on Billie, supposedly totting up how much she drank every week based on the flimsiest of reports from 'fellow pub guests' and all the usual 'insiders' at celebrity functions.

Perhaps it should have been no surprise, then, that some commentators got back on Billie's case. What depressed her was that they often dragged her parents into their arguments, even though Mandy and Paul had already said how happy they were for their daughter. One final example of the running criticism came in June. 'What must Billie Piper's mum and dad be thinking this week?' was how the *Sunday Mirror* began its latest commentary. 'In the two months since their daughter married Chris Evans – a wedding to which they weren't invited – they have watched their little girl change from a stunningly beautiful 18-year-old with a glittering pop career into a messy, unkempt girl who, on a good day, could pass for a dosser. This young woman, who before she met Evans had the ability to light up a room, now skulks around London with dirty hair, no make-up and baggy clothes. She never smiles and rarely gets up before midday on account of the fact she and her new husband have been out all night drinking. This week, their sad little marriage hit the headlines again with reports of one 18-hour bender where a drunken Evans flirted with Lady Victoria Hervey, leaving his child bride to run home in tears.'

As the accusations, lies, exaggerations and rumours built up, Billie felt herself thrown forcibly back into a world she thought she had left. It was as if she was 16 again, being falsely accused by the press of having a drug habit, an unwanted pregnancy and even an illicit abortion. At the time, her parents and younger siblings were in the final stages of following their dream of living in Spain. If they did so, it would at least partly shield Mandy and Paul from the latest set of false and hurtful headlines about their daughter's 'tragic decline' and 'wasted life'. Chris, who needed to read every newspaper every day to keep his breakfast show topical and funny, had found his own way to avoid the negative press. He asked his team at Virgin Radio to cut out any critical articles about himself and his wife before passing the papers on to him. Billie, however, didn't want to read pages with huge gaps in them – not least because worst-case scenarios of what might have been printed would prey on her mind for the rest of the day. She needed another way to escape from all the depressing commentaries. But how could she?

She and Chris started to talk more and more about leaving Britain altogether and starting sunnier, low-pressure lives somewhere far away. It was a fantastically appealing prospect, not least because the pair had always been happiest either out of London or out of the country. But two big obstacles stood in their way – both had work to do in Britain and, as the summer heated up, Billie knew she had to wrest back control of her career.

The long-awaited fourth single from *Walk of Life* had still not been released. Billie had persuaded Innocent to hold fire until the weather got better, but now that the sun was shining, everyone had to decide what to do. As the first sets of meetings got under way, rumours of big problems started to surface. For a start, Virgin pulled the plug on Billie's official website in the summer. The public line was that it was simply being updated and would be back brighter, better and more functional than ever in the autumn – hopefully with news of a new album and possibly even a British tour. The open secret, however, was that the fansite was being shut down due to lack of interest. Meanwhile, the third album and a touring schedule were the big topics of conversation in the Innocent boardroom. Everyone agreed that Billie's career was at a crossroads. Her grown-up re-launch as Billie Piper had been done superbly – winning her new, older fans without losing her former market among pre-teen girls. But it seemed that this strategy was being undermined by Billie's personal life. Going out with Ritchie Neville had brought its own highly public set of problems; being married to Chris Evans had brought a new batch of issues to the table.

'In a nutshell, it is simple – being with someone as old as Chris Evans has put off all of Billie's little girl fans. They just didn't want to be her any more because they just don't want to be with him,' said one industry adviser candidly. 'Billie is losing her fan base because of her association with Chris Evans. Even the older fans no longer see her as cool now she is married to someone old enough to be her and their father.'

The fans that Billie did still have – and there were many who messaged each other on several unofficial supporters' sites – were arguing about whether 'Ring My Bell' or 'Bring It On' should get released as a single. Many, though, thought that as so long had now passed since *Walk of Life*'s poor showing, a better thing would be to start a new album with a clean slate. Hugh Goldsmith, the man who had found and launched Billie two years ago, was coming to the same conclusion. But when he and Billie finally sat down and had a serious discussion, he realised this was unlikely ever to happen. She told him that, deep down, she wanted to break free of her obligation to record another album. Her heart wasn't in it. And without that, he knew that nothing she recorded would be worth releasing.

With as little fanfare as possible, Innocent first put Billie's contract into a 'holding pattern' on the understanding that the final album could still be made at some undisclosed point in the future. After less than a few months, however, this fig leaf of protection would be removed and it was pretty much agreed that Billie wasn't going back into any studio. Billie Piper, the record breaker who had had more Number Ones at a younger age than anyone else in pop history, was giving up the role that had made her famous.

At first, all Billie felt was relief. She was finally free to admit that pop music had never been her life goal, that she had been doing a job rather than following her dreams every time she stood in front of a microphone. After a while, though, she would come to miss some elements of the music world. Writing and recording songs had been something she had enjoyed; rehearsing dance routines and performing on stage had been fun and making videos had felt a little bit like being in Hollywood. But Billie knew full well that she couldn't take the good bits without the bad. And the bad part was the endless, exhausting promotion she always had to do to sell the music – the soul-destroying mix of interviews, guest appearances, two-track gigs and false smiles.

When it was clear that her contract was ending, one of the first people Billie spoke to after Chris was her mother. She knew that Mandy had always been wrongly described as being a classic example of the pushy parent who had driven her daughter into the spotlight to make up for her own supposedly failed career. And Billie knew that Mandy would support her in any decision she took to move on. Mandy then proved it, with a damning critique of the music industry as a whole. 'Billie has hardly had any time to stop and think, so it is wonderful she is now able to do both. All the travelling round, all the endless promotion just dragged her down. The way record companies market and promote these youngsters is very tough, pushing them into the limelight day after day. Half the time, these young stars – and Billie was far from the only one – don't even know what time of day it is. It has been so fraught for Billie over the past few years and, if she now needs a rest and a break, we want her to have it.'

Fiercely proud of her daughter, Mandy couldn't resist answering the critics with a final reminder of Billie's achievements. 'Yes, Billie has grown up very fast — perhaps too fast — which is sad because, in a way, she has missed out on a part of her childhood. But at least she has already done something big with her life and can look back and say she has achieved something.'

As usual, not everyone was prepared to be this generous, however. Billie's departure from the music scene made it on to the stand-up circuit and the news review shows on television. 'Billie Piper has just said she is fed up with being a pop star... We were fed up with her being a pop star three years ago,' was how her retirement was presented on *Have I Got News For You?* for example.

As everyone would soon find out, it wasn't just Billie who was going through something of a mid-career crisis in the summer of 2001. Chris was also finding it increasingly hard to stay inspired at work. He and Billie were living for their time off and their nights out — Billie called them a 'double act' when they hit their local pubs in London and Surrey. But as the weeks passed and they settled into their new married life, this very social double act was going to trigger some seriously expensive repercussions at Virgin Radio.

Chris's history in radio had made him one of the biggest stars in broadcasting — and most of this was inextricably linked to Virgin. He had begun his radio career there back in 1993 when the station had been owned by Richard Branson. Two years later, it had been with Radio One that his real talent for the medium started to reveal itself. His skilfully anarchic, team-based approach to the breakfast show revolutionised the market and made the station essential listening after several years in the doldrums. In 1997, Chris — and most of his production team — jumped ship and went back to Virgin where audience figures and advertising revenues soon started to soar. Contracted to present four shows a week, Chris often turned up and hosted five or even six. And, in December, he presented his biggest shock to date — slipping ahead of radio rival Capital and buying Virgin from Sir Richard for £83 million. His new incarnation as an extraordinarily successful media mogul had begun, and he had also found a way to get seriously rich. Within less than three years, he sold the station and his Ginger production company to Scottish Media Group for a staggering £225 million, while retaining a multi-million pound contract to continue with his breakfast broadcasts and continuing with his equally successful family of television shows.

This had been the state of play when Billie had entered his life. And soon afterwards, the cracks had begun to show. The first of them became apparent just before Chris and Billie flew off to America and got married. Chris had been increasingly unhappy with several members of his breakfast crew, so they were let go while he was out of the country. After coming back to Britain, and with a fresh team in place, the Virgin breakfast show looked set for a total return to form. And, ironically enough, its first set of problems came about because Chris wanted to work more, rather than less.

On 6 June, the day of England's vital World Cup qualifier against Greece, Chris was hosting the show with his chief wedding guest John Webster. Everyone thought the show had gone brilliantly and the team was on a real roll as they entered the final half-hour of the broadcast. So why not stay on air all day? Chris and Webbo demanded the chance to do just that – but the executives at SMG said no. An impasse was reached, before Chris's studio was taken off the air amidst some very public recriminations.

At this point, it was clear that a host of other pressures had been building up – and it was equally clear just why Billie and Chris saw themselves as soulmates. Her disillusionment with music, the thing which had made her famous, was exactly mirrored by his disillusionment with radio. Both were simultaneously desperate for escape – and despite the widespread belief that they were some mismatched odd couple, they were utterly in sync. By the summer of 2001, when Billie had negotiated her break with Innocent, she had taken her first steps towards freedom. Chris was about to follow in her footsteps.

Full details of his exact route wouldn't really be revealed for a couple of years, after Chris had been ousted from Virgin Radio, and he took his former employer to court for unfair dismissal. In June 2001, all the station's early-morning listeners knew was that Chris was no longer on air every day. The papers ramped up their coverage of his supposed booze benders, and he was phoning in sick and saying he couldn't present his show as normal.

One evening, he and Billie were seen at their London regular, The Nag's Head, and the papers reported that over the course of six hours they drank everything from lagers and cider to Bloody Marys, whiskies and vodkas with Red Bull, ultimately running out of cash and having to set up a tab.

On Thursday, 21 June, Billie rang Chris's agent, Michael Foster, to say Chris wouldn't be doing the next morning's show. And over the next few days, the pattern continued. The media became even more obsessed with the way the pair were spending their days – and nights – and a battalion of photographers were despatched to follow their every move. So when they left the Waitrose supermarket in Godalming pushing a trolley loaded up with yet more booze, the pictures made all the front pages the following day. As did all the details.

It turned out that Chris and Billie had bought 24 cans of Fosters, 12 cans of Carlsberg, five bottles of French Chardonnay and a bottle of Australian Cabernet Sauvignon. 'They also collected a few groceries and some Diet Coke,' added the *Daily Mail* dryly.

Not surprisingly, the management at Virgin Radio owner SMG were getting increasingly frustrated by the actions of their star performer. He was certainly giving the station a seemingly endless amount of free publicity, but most of the top brass would have preferred to have him presenting his show. At home, though, Chris was under a huge amount of pressure, with Billie doing all she could to help. They called in his GP, Doctor John Gayner, who said he was 'chronically stressed' and could not stop crying.

It was around this time that Billie took on a new identity in her marriage. They were having great fun – even climbing through The Nag's Head window early one morning to make themselves a coffee before opening time. But Billie was also genuinely worried about her husband. So as the days passed, her hidden steel came into its own. She prepared to take on the role of protector and guide for her new husband – a change of dynamic which the experts said would either make or break the Evans marriage.

'Often different partners are in charge of relationships at different times and this can sometimes add extra dangers,' explains Oxford-based marriage guidance therapist Emilia Edgar. 'If the partner who had traditionally dominated proceedings is suddenly pushed into a secondary role, then their feelings of insecurity can cause real problems. On a positive note, if the couple get through the crisis without feeling any jealousy and with a new sense of working as a team, then the relationship can be even stronger.'

Billie and Chris would soon prove that Team Evans

had acquired premiership status after the events of this summer. But before this happened, the endgame in the Virgin Radio drama was still to be played out.

This came at 3.25pm on Thursday, 28 June 2001. Chris had missed five shows in a row and Virgin Radio decided to take action. It announced that Chris was in breach of his contract and that the company had no option but to terminate it. As an aside, SMG made it clear that the third tranche of shares due to Chris as part of his 2000 sale of the station would not now be paid. If this threat was followed through, it would cost Chris some £8 million. Closure looked set to be an expensive and distant prospect as a war of words began over the biggest radio-based news story of the year.

Behind the scenes, the unlikely truth was that Chris's exit from Virgin Radio had done wonders for his and Billie's relationship. Both had now got shot of the huge career anchors that had been dragging them down for too long. Both were now facing a future where they were finally free to do what they wanted, rather than what showbusiness logic dictated. Most importantly, both were now ready for a new set of joint adventures. They were going to go on holiday… and they told friends that they might be some time.

8
BILLIE HOLIDAY

BILLIE AND CHRIS didn't just head into the sunset after slaying their career demons in the summer of 2001. They headed into an endless series of sunsets – normally ones they could view from the comfort of five-star resorts around the world. It was the slightly delayed start of what would be dubbed the longest – and arguably the booziest – honeymoon in history. Billie and Chris had both been working solidly since leaving school. Suddenly it was payback time... they were going to have a ball.

Their first big stop was Florida, where they stayed for nearly a month. Best Man Danny Baker and his family flew out to join them for a while and the group became theme park and roller-coaster experts as they joined the tourist throngs and tried to fight off the muggy, mid-summer heat. Billie tipped Orlando's Universal Islands of Adventure as her favourite, although the water rides at Blizzard Beach came a close second as the temperature mounted.

After Florida, Billie and Chris headed west to stay at the Sunset Marquis hotel in Los Angeles. Just off Sunset Boulevard, the hotel describes itself as 'unique, even by Hollywood standards', and lists a state-of-the-art recording studio and screening room alongside all its other guest services. 'Rock star to your left, famous actress to your right. You are either at the Sunset Marquis or at a treatment centre. If we were any more Hollywood, our pool would be shallow at both ends,' is how Robbie Williams' favourite LA hotel likes to describe itself. Billie and Chris thought it was all hilarious — and fantastic. After some low-key star-spotting, they just chilled out in a private cabana beside the largest of the two pools and got a taste for the city they would soon call home.

Billie spent a lot of her time subtly checking up on her husband's state of mind — just as she had done since they had left Britain nearly two months earlier. She felt she was one step ahead of Chris in the life-change stakes, and had taken a far less dramatic leap out of her former existence. They both talked endlessly about the pressures they had been under — admitting, often for the very first time, just how unhappy they had been before they had met.

'I was desperate… absolutely desperate,' Chris said of his mindset when he and Billie had first begun dating.

'People think that having the kind of lifestyle I had and being that famous is amazing, but I was so totally unhappy. I was out all the time, surrounded by all these people, doing whatever I wanted. But I remember looking at all these friends around me and realising that most of them were on my payroll. The problem was that I was actually a pretty normal bloke and, because of that, I had no idea how to handle things. I know now that it's not good to get everything you want. In fact, it was pretty horrible. I didn't need a psychiatrist to tell me what was wrong with me and I didn't need anyone to tell me what to do about it. It just got to the point where I knew I had to get off the ride, stop everything and walk away.'

It turned out to be exactly the right thing to do. 'The moment I walked away was the moment I started to get better,' Chris added. 'It was instantaneous. Getting out of that mad, intense whirl was the only thing I could do to stay sane.'

The wonderful thing was that all those same sentiments – indeed, the same words – could have come from Billie's mouth as well as from Chris. They were two people damaged by living in the public eye, trying to repair themselves in a closed, almost Garbo-esque world. They wanted to be alone – or at least alone together. So, as they sat under the Californian sun, they celebrated just how alike they were, and just how perfectly their other qualities and life experiences made their relationship stronger. 'There was Billie's innocence, which I needed, and my experience, which she needed, and we sort of joined them together,' is how Chris saw it. The end result was something far stronger than their critics back in Britain could have ever imagined.

Not that Billie and Chris had much intention of coming back to Britain for some time. After deciding they were ready to leave LA for a while, their next major stop was Portugal. And they weren't going to just spend time there – they had decided to spend some serious money as well.

Chris's love of golf made the Algarve a perfect spot for him and he was keen to try and get Billie into the sport as well. A villa on the edge of a golf course, therefore, seemed in order and the couple decided there would be no half measures as they sought out the best. First, Chris picked what he reckoned was the best golf course – the Joseph Lee-designed San Lorenzo sandwiched between the ocean and the Ria Formosa National Park. Next, they wanted the best villa – which was when they hit a snag. They were shown a great property on the exclusive Quinta Do Lago estate, but weren't sure if it was really big enough for them. So in their new 'anything's possible' mood, they decided to put in an offer for the villa next door as well and convert them both into one spectacular home. The total bill, including the building work, was set to come in at an eye-watering £2.5 million.

Billie and Chris decided to go for it. It was the first property they had bought together as a couple, and they were excited about starting a new chapter of their lives.

Billie's dad Paul was brought in to supervise the reconstruction work, travelling over from the Pipers' new home in Mijas, Spain. But however much money they were spending on their dream home, Billie and Chris retained their common touches. Most nights they shunned the ritzy restaurants and bars of the nearby five-star hotels. Instead, they were far more likely to be found eating seafood and rice in far-flung fishing villages, stopping off and becoming regulars at local bars such as Rumours, Hero's and the Pig and Whistle on their way home.

In the daytime, Billie hadn't caught the golfing bug, despite Chris's best efforts. But while he and his friends worked on their handicaps, she was more than happy to lie by the pool topping up her tan and recharging her batteries. Having finally had the time to take her driving test, she happily scooted around the local villages in a green, open-topped Jaguar sports car, taking her time buying bread, milk and fruit and enjoying the unexpected pleasure of total anonymity.

'I was just happy and relaxed, reading books, learning about who I was,' she says of the experience. 'At that age, you don't know who you are. I had found a soul-mate who would let me breathe and let me explore that side of myself as he explored the other sides of him. Yes, I was being completely selfish, but I felt like I needed to be. And I also felt that I had earned the right to have some time out to do exactly what I wanted to do for a change. I had gone straight from school into a full-blown career and I never really got the chance to have those lazy days. I just need to do some normal things – to stay in bed for a whole day, to watch movies back to back for three days, to treat myself to some Häagen-Dazs. I've missed life,' she said, as she took full advantage of her bid to catch up.

To her credit, Billie was well aware of the uniqueness of her situation and of her overall good fortune. In a world where most people work to survive, she and Chris would never take their new freedoms for granted. 'How do you cope with each other's bad moods?' a reporter asked her during the first half of the couple's extended honeymoon period. Billie was totally honest in her reply. 'We're very rarely in bad moods. There's no reason for us to be in bad moods. If everyone was as lucky as us, they would very rarely fight either,' she replied – a world away from the self-pitying attitude struck by many of her fellow celebrities.

Billie was keeping her feet on the ground in other ways as well. On a break from overseas luxury, they headed back to Britain and she took Chris to the Isle of Wight and a caravan park in Ewell, Surrey, where she re-lived some of her childhood memories to explain more about who she was. The pair also put down deep roots elsewhere in Surrey, back at Hascombe Court. Chris's long-standing renovation and renewal project had continued apace while he and Billie had been abroad, and Billie in particular loved the challenge of sourcing and organising some of the finishing touches. Estate agents and valuers who visited the property said the work had been done incredibly sensitively – for Billie and Chris there was no rock star excess, just painstaking and well-researched attention to detail.

They shared the house with two others – their lurchers Percy and Epstein – and they would gradually build up a wider menagerie which included donkeys, sheep, rabbits and goats. The couple also tried to grow organic vegetables which Billie, having mastered the art of making a decent curry, tried to use in her own kitchen.

Billie was the first to admit that she would have laughed out loud five years ago if anyone had told her that by 2001 she would be married, no longer working, living in the sticks and happily learning to cook. She had certainly never seen herself as a country housewife at 19 years old. But then she had never been more relaxed – so some good karma was certainly in the air.

For all this quiet domestic bliss, Mr and Mrs Evans didn't quite live like monks at their country retreat. The White Horse pub is the hub of nearby Haslemere, and so it became the hub of Billie and Chris's lives when they were staying at Hascombe Court. Having already got to know the landlord well, they also became close friends with the regulars and spent night after night drinking the Adnam's Ale Chris was always hoping to find in LA or Portugal. Most of the other regulars at the White Horse were older than Chris, let alone Billie, but she found herself liberated rather than suffocated by the atmosphere there. 'When you talk to famous people, everyone is dull and guarded and terrified about not letting their masks slip and there's no point to it,' she said. 'But the conversations in our local pub are so interesting because they are real and they are about real things. The people we know there have hobbies, they do things with their weekends. We've got a friend who is a bee keeper; another one who is in pest control, and everyone just has great stories. I learn things there. It's a real education because it is not about work or ego, ego, ego. It's not about who has the most money and who has slept with who. It's like, I want to tell you about my new bee-catching device and all the other things which make up ordinary life.'

And despite cynics saying this was some sort of Marie Antoinette syndrome on Billie's part — the rich sophisticate craving an unrealistically simple life — friends say she did genuinely thrive in her new world. And many of the closest friends she made there have stuck to this day.

Billie's car in Surrey was equally down to earth. The open-top Jag was in Portugal and Chris preferred to drive the Ferrari he had bought his wife less than a year previously (he would ultimately emerge unscathed after driving it into a ditch on the way to the gym early one morning). So Billie was happy to keep a low profile in a nippy little Renault Clio.

With Christmas coming, Billie got one big reminder of just how much her life had changed in the past 12 months. A year ago, she had been on a London balcony in front of thousands of shoppers as she switched on the

Top: Billie enjoys watching the tennis at the Queen's Club, London.

Below left: The funeral at Hascombe, Surrey, of James Ward, who died in a sailing accident whilst with friends Chris and Billie.

Below right: At the Baftas in early 2004.

Billie has seen her fair share of courtroom dramas. Above, flanked by her father Paul, the singer leaves Blackfriars Crown Court, after giving evidence in the trial of a 'fan' accused of having made threats to kill her in August 2000; and below, she leaves court after Chris was found guilty of speeding in May 2001.

Billie accidentally reveals a little too much while on stage at G.A.Y., London!

Spot the difference: the humble flats in Swindon where Billie first lived, and Hascombe Court, the country estate she shared with husband Chris.

Billie out and about with her current beau, Amadu Sowe, whom she first met at Innocent Records.

Billie in classic Rose pose, filming the primetime 2005 *Doctor Who* Christmas special – she brought action, style and humour to her role.

Billie enjoyed great screen chemistry with the two charismatic Doctors Who, Christopher Eccleston and his successor David Tennant.

80

Billie lines up with *Doctor Who* writer Russell T. Davies and David Tennant at the Baftas, where the programme won Best Serial Drama. Billie achieved great recognition for her turn as the Doctor's sidekick, a role she relinquished after her second series.

Regent Street Christmas lights. In December 2001, she and Chris pulled on red Father Christmas hats and set up a stall outside their local pub. They were selling Christmas trees from their grounds to help raise money for their local church repairs, a cystic fibrosis charity and a Surrey hospice. It was a cold, crisp day and business was slow for the first couple of hours the couple stood out there. At one point, Chris put his hands inside Billie's gloves to try and warm up her fingers and they both stomped around the pub car park to try and keep the blood moving. Billie said it was the start of one of the nicest Christmases she could remember since she had been a tiny girl. Back in London, the tenor Russell Watson was following in Billie's footsteps by turning on the 2001 Regent Street lights. Billie didn't envy him for a second.

After celebrating the New Year alone together, the pair were soon back at Heathrow. In early 2002, they headed back to Los Angeles – their extended honeymoon was continuing apace. 'There is absolutely nothing in his diary. He is on holiday and we don't know if he will come back. Who knows?' a spokesman for Chris's PR firm, Freud Communications, told the media as questions started to be asked about how such a career-focused and ambitious man seemed to have fallen below the entertainment radar. 'I'm on a 100-day holiday. Come back to me at the end of it,' he had told his agent, jokingly, after first setting off on his travels with Billie. And this wasn't all. 'I liked the 100 days so much that I awarded myself another 100,' he said after crossing that first milestone. He and Billie still quite understandably saw themselves as among the luckiest people alive.

This year, though, their time in LA wasn't to be spent just resting beside a hotel pool. The couple had decided they ought to buy a house in the City of Angels, and the process was going to be fantastic fun from start to finish. 'Whatever level of the market you are at, buying property in America is quite different to buying it in Britain. And buying at the level Billie and Chris had reached is different to almost anywhere else in the world,' says Laurel Canyon real estate broker Roseanna Zuckerman. 'What makes it special is that you really do need to prove your worth to be taken seriously by an agent – it is not something your average tourist can do by turning up and faking interest in a multi-million dollar home. But once an agent knows you've got the cash, you're going to be treated like the closest thing America gets to royalty.' According to Roseanna, real estate agents in LA are likely to drive clients to properties in anything from a limo or a Lexus to a classic Rolls-Royce. And in the multi-million dollar market, the properties they will see will be just as eye-watering.

Billie and Chris saw their fair share of stunners in those late winter days when the LA sky was clear and the dry Santa Ana winds pushed temperatures up towards the seventies. But one property had that little bit of extra magic. Lionel Ritchie had built it high in the Hollywood Hills just after hitting the top of the charts with 'Easy' and 'Three Times a Lady'. Described by locals as a 'gingerbread palace', it had five sprawling bedrooms, took up some 6,000 square feet and had a swimming pool, tennis court and guest house in its private, leafy grounds. It also had a stiff £5.6 million price tag – but by the time they found this out, Billie and Chris were sold.

'We looked at loads of houses but came back to this one several times before deciding it was the one we wanted. We wanted somewhere with a great view and the whole area here is great. Who wouldn't want to live here?' asked Warrington-born Chris as he bought into the LA lifestyle.

As it turned out, Billie and Chris weren't the only ones wanting to live in the house, however. After they moved in, they found a mini-colony of rats was sharing the long-empty mansion with them. So a Hollywood pest control team was their first main visitor. After that, the couple moved back into their joint shell. They might have been in the entertainment capital of the world, but most nights they simply stayed at home, more often than not watching old Morecambe & Wise and Monty Python videos in the warm Californian evenings.

They became regulars at furniture stores in Beverly Hills as they tried to fill all their big new LA rooms, and spent hours wandering anonymously around junk and antique stores in Santa Monica. They also went to classic car auctions, leafed through the old vinyl collections at downtown record shops, even hit a few strikes at some of the town's typically glitzy bowling alleys. Best of all, they did almost all of this totally undisturbed. It seemed that the British paparazzi had finally given up on seeking the killer photo of the pair looking either drunkenly happy or depressingly sad. And the American snappers didn't seem to know or care who they were – which was just the way Billie liked it.

In all, it was an idyllic life. 'We would go for a coffee and the papers every morning, relax and decide what we were going to do for the day. We used to go to the cinema a lot and we ate really healthily,' Chris said. Both started working out at a nearby gym and Billie tried her hand at yoga. She also took on some of her husband's perhaps surprising interests – reading the Dalai Lama, Bertrand Russell, philosophy and self-help books while sitting under a palm tree in her garden.

'We are now the idle rich,' Chris joked to old friends from home who asked what the couple did every day. They were also utterly secure in their marriage – Billie, in particular, being convinced that their 'mega-break' honeymoon was laying fantastic foundations for their future. 'So many relationships don't work out because couples don't have enough time together at the beginning,' was her theory. 'The way Chris and I have done things, it feels as if we have been mates for ever and I much prefer that to the temporary feeling, when you like someone but you don't know if they are going to be there when you get home. I like feeling settled at home and with Chris, I do.'

With this in mind, it should have been little surprise when the couple's first wedding anniversary came around and their relationship was still very much intact. To try and rebuild bridges with her parents, Billie made sure she and Chris flew back across the Atlantic and had a family party just before the big day. They then flew back to their Hollywood home and celebrated in typically unique style. The first thing that happened on the night in question was that they drove through their security gates in an eye-catching white Mustang convertible. But it turned out that they weren't off to Spago, The Ivy, the Mondrian or any of the city's other hot celebrity restaurants. Instead, they just drove as far as their local Indian restaurant where they picked up a takeaway and headed straight back home to eat it.

Back in Swindon, Billie's mum laughed at the news and said it was utterly in keeping with her daughter's wonderfully relaxed new life. 'I never had any doubt that she and Chris would make their first wedding anniversary. They are very happy and I am very happy for Billie,' Mandy said. 'Billie wasn't happy for quite a long time and now she is. For my part, I definitely feel she is safer under Chris's wing and he is looking after her very well.'

When Billie was asked for any marriage secrets after notching up her first anniversary, she said it was the little things which made a difference. 'What I love about Chris is the way we both see things. Sometimes, I will see something and if I tell someone else they are going to laugh at it or just not get it. Not everyone will understand or think it is important. But Chris will.'

On a more profound note, it was clear that she had also given a lot of thought to the way relationships work – although she admitted she hadn't always come up with all the answers. 'I have never asked Chris why he married me,' she said. 'He knows what he likes and what he wants and you just have to trust that. Sometimes, I'll do something that will surprise him and it is nice not to know what that might be because you will end up playing on that. If someone says, "I really like the way you hold your cigarette," then every time you meet someone new you are going to be hoping you can charm them with your cigarette act. So I don't think I want to know.'

For Billie, the girl who had always been looking and planning ahead, it was finally possible to live in the moment.

9
COUNTRY LIFE AND COURT CASES

IN THE SUMMER of 2002, Billie and Chris decided to escape the heat of LA and were back spending plenty of time in Hascombe Court. And within days of their return, they slotted comfortably back into the heart of that close-knit local community. Chris was helping to set up a village cricket team and build a new cricket pavilion; Billie was swapping holiday stories at The White Hart, as happy to hear about other people's two weeks in Spain as she was to talk about her two months in California and elsewhere. Meanwhile, she even followed her husband to Lord's to watch her first ever cricket match, and while Chris had also given her something of a taste for football (pretty important in a World Cup summer) she admitted that golf remained pretty much a total turn-off.

The only problem the couple had when they came

back to Britain for the summer was that they were in danger of inadvertently edging back into the media spotlight. Something as innocent and ordinary as drinking in the garden of their local pub or wandering around the nearby supermarket could get the photographers interested and trigger a new wave of comment about their lifestyles.

The pub photographs were the first to bring a response, although the shopping shots would be a lot more personal. Years later, Billie looked back at the media obsession with their drinking and said she simply couldn't understand it. 'The drinking was never an issue. I never thought either of us ever had a problem. Friends go to university and drink solidly for three years. We weren't doing anything that other people don't do, apart from having some time off. For my part, I don't drink to dull things or numb any pain. I just do it socially because it's a laugh. And Chris is not some kind of pub bore drunk who'd start fights. He's a really cheerful, funny drunk.'

Chef and friend Aldo Zilli also spoke up, refuting the suggestions that Chris was somehow leading Billie astray with a string of pub crawls. 'Chris is not an alcoholic, he can take or leave alcohol and, on many occasions, he has not been drinking while the rest of us have. The idea that he forces people around him to drink is utterly ridiculous.'

Equally ridiculous and far more hurtful were the implications several papers drew from a handful of unflattering pictures of Billie at the local shops; 'a bigger

Billie' was one singularly unimaginative caption that summer. Other papers then took the idea further: 'DESPERATE BILLIE POPS SLIM PILLS' was the worst of the unfounded accusations as Billie's supposed weight problems pushed a host of other stories out of the papers. What bothered Billie the most about this new trend in her public profile was that she had always been proud of her position as a role model for ordinary girls and young women. Despite a few typically teenage crises when she had spent too long looking at super-thin pop colleagues, she had always been determined not to fall into any self-esteem or anorexia neuroses. In everything she had said and done, she had tried to get this message across to others.

'I'm never going to be some supermodel rake and I can't say I want to be. I'm big-boned, I'm average size and weight... and I love burgers and chips,' she said with refreshing honesty. The idea that she would go against all this and try quack cures to lose weight was damaging on all sorts of levels. Billie and Chris – who had anyway pretty much stopped reading the tabloid papers altogether – felt they could shake off the false stories. But Billie knew her mother might worry if she read it, and she was furious at the message it might send out to the papers' young readers. But what could she do?

'Never complain, never explain.' The four-word mantra is the one that allegedly served everyone from Benjamin Disraeli, Henry Ford and Jackie Kennedy to the Queen. The thinking behind it is that if you take issue with one story written about you, then you have to take issue over them all — because after your first set of complaints, people will think that anything you don't comment on must be true. The argument goes that it is far better to just keep your head down, carry on with your life and refuse to dignify your critics with any responses. When Chris had left Virgin the previous year, his PR team had been approached with more than 700 requests for interviews. All had been turned down. One year on, Billie knew she had to keep the same low profile over the latest set of rumours about her mental and physical health. She accepted that she was still strangely newsworthy — though this did seem bizarre after more than a year out of the public eye when she had done all she could think of to keep out of the media's way.

One part of her life which was never made public was the way Billie had coped with some of the personal baggage that came with being Chris's second wife. Not everyone would have been comfortable knowing their husband had a daughter just four years younger than them. But Billie had taken this fact in her stride from the start and she was happy to have Chris's ex-wife Alison and his daughter Jade round to stay at Hascombe Court. Jade said Billie was particularly welcoming and the unlikely foursome had a surprisingly relaxed few days together, although, perhaps understandably, no lifelong friendships were born.

In a bid to stay in the shadows, Billie and Chris didn't have to think twice when they were approached about taking part in a celebrity episode of *Wife Swap* that summer (the producers had wanted them to switch lives with Richard and Judy). They said 'no' without a moment's hesitation and, with Richard and Judy equally unwilling to take part, the way was left clear for Jade Goody and Jeff Brazier to do the swap with *Who Wants to Be A Millionaire?*'s coughing Major Charles Ingram and his wife Diana.

Dark clouds gathered when tragedy struck Billie and Chris's village in August — the lowest point of an otherwise wonderful year. The pair had joined a big group from Haslemere on the Isle of Wight to celebrate the 55th birthday of Sue Barnett, the business partner of their pub landlord James Ward. James was a keen sailor and he and several of the group were out on the Solent aboard *Nausicaa* enjoying the late summer winds when an accident occurred. He was hit by the boom of the yacht and knocked unconscious into the water. Neither the crew on *Nausicaa* nor the emergency services were able to revive him and he was pronounced dead at the scene.

On 19 August, Billie and Chris left the gates to their house and walked half-a-mile, hand in hand, to the local church where more than 300 mourners had gathered for James's funeral. In the event, more than 100 people had to remain outside St Peter's Church to hear the 45-minute service relayed on hastily-erected loudspeakers. Then the White Horse regulars headed back to James's old pub for a wake. As they joined them, Billie and Chris were both devastated that their own fame meant reporters and photographers had gathered in the village to witness the end of this very private, local tragedy. 'You heard it all in the church. I haven't anything else to add,' Chris told the journalists who pressed the pair for comments on their way back into the village. He and Billie pulled each other closer as they walked, fully aware once more of just how fortunate their lives were and how lucky they had been to find each other.

Perhaps in response to the tragedy in Haslemere, Billie and Chris spent much of the rest of the year cocooned even closer within each other's lives. The media was finally off their backs and most of the time no one knew whether they were in Britain, Portugal, Los Angeles or anywhere else. They were happy, though, living increasingly ordinary lives, shopping for groceries, dealing with builders and decorators and putting down roots around the world.

Their one underlying worry was the preparation Chris was having to do for his next moment in the spotlight. In the early spring of 2003, he was due to face Virgin Radio in court over his departure from the station two years earlier. At issue, among many other things, would be the estimated £8.6 million of share options that had been withheld from him that summer. At stake could be his entire professional reputation.

Just before the case began, Billie and Chris flew to Barbados where they stayed at the Sandy Lane Hotel. Sitting under the mahogany trees and gazing out over the white-sand beaches, the pair spent almost all their time together, according to fellow guests. Chris was no longer leaving Billie alone all day while he played golf. Instead, they idled away their days in contented, companionable silence, holding hands and occasionally dipping into the ocean or the freshwater swimming pool. 'If you hadn't known different, you would have said that this was their honeymoon,' one fellow holidaymaker told the papers afterwards. Indeed, Billie told friends that she was still so happy with Chris that it sometimes felt as if they had only just met.

So this made it all the stranger that, back in London, a new assault had begun on the Evans' marriage. A rash of stories sprang up saying the pair were in trouble, that Billie was unhappy, and that Chris was uncertain about the future. Obviously, no facts were available to back up any of the false rumours. But there were several theories about why they were being spread. Some people suggested a smear campaign was being brought to coincide with the forthcoming court case – although no one had any clear idea of who might be behind the campaign or what its purpose might be. Chris's press spokesman Matthew Freud (who had had precious little to do during his client's extended break from public life) did take action that spring, however. He wrote to every national newspaper editor saying false stories were being planted about supposed problems in the Evans's marriage. 'Someone is putting it about that the marriage is over. It is rubbish. They are fine and the marriage is fine. It couldn't be better,' said one of Freud's colleagues after a long conversation with the couple.

The case would ultimately last seven weeks and began at the High Court in London with several weeks of legal arguments between the two sides. At issue was Chris's claim for the share options he had not received, and Scottish Media Group's counter claim alleging breach of contract. When the initial legal arguments had been resolved and the case proper began, Billie and Chris were to see a great deal of their dirty laundry being washed in public. A huge amount of the case was spent discussing the drinking sessions Chris had gone on after meeting Billie and the trip to America they had made when they had got married. Chris was often close to tears when giving evidence, with Billie distracted and upset as she watched from the other side of the courtroom.

But for all the stresses and strains, there were several lighter moments. Geoffrey Vos QC was the man representing SMG and one day he referred to Chris as 'a talented radio presenter'.

'I don't know if everyone in the court accepts that but, yes, I would agree with you,' Chris interrupted, to the laughter of the court.

'I had not seen anyone so frightening since I looked at myself in the mirror six years ago,' Chris said on another occasion after discussing one of the station's programme directors.

In the midst of the crisis in 2001, Vos repeated a

comment from Chris's agent Michael Foster that the star had been 'in a dark place'.

'I was in a very dark place,' Chris agreed.

'A pub?' ventured Vos.

'I was going to say that but I didn't want to appear flippant in court,' Chris replied to more laughter from the crowded public gallery.

The jokes had long since stopped by the time the summing up had begun, though, and when the verdict came on 26 June, Billie and Chris were both in for some very sober moments. Chris had lost his case; he had failed to win back his share options or win any money for unfair dismissal. He also looked set to face a massive bill for damages and costs, though this was ultimately scaled down to a still hefty £1 million.

What he did have to face was an extraordinarily tough description of his personality and his behaviour from the judge, Mr Justice Lightman. 'As in a Greek tragedy, the eventual outcome was practically inevitable,' he said in his lengthy judgement on the case. He said Chris was 'an unimpressive witness, more concerned with advocacy and making an impression than answering questions'. Worse, the judge described Chris as 'petulant and given to sulking and walking away from situations whenever he considers himself thwarted. He is not ready to make concessions to others. He is a person who cannot tolerate either criticism or the exercise by management of authority over what he does.' Finally, the old issue of alcohol was raised. 'He is given to extremes – moderation has no part to play,' said the judge. 'Drinking to excess is part of his lifestyle… He told me with pride and no trace of embarrassment that, more often than not, he presented the show with a hangover.'

Billie and Chris hadn't been in court to hear the ruling, although Chris issued a brief and enigmatic statement – 'All will come out right at last – have we such faith in the goodness of providence'– which was based on an exchange between Henry Stanley and the missionary David Livingstone in Africa.

He also shrugged off the financial implications of the defeat telling the *News of the World*, 'It's only money. I still have it in the bank.' He also continued to have Billie's full support. She certainly hadn't recognised the man described in court as the man she lived with and loved. The financial implications of losing the case were equally irrelevant to Billie – just as they were to Chris.

Shortly after the verdict, some ridiculous rumours sprung up over the amount the couple had allegedly been spending since their 2001 marriage. Chris, estimated to be worth £77 million in the late 1990s, was now pegged at 'just' £25 million and had supposedly crashed out of the top ten of Britain's richest broadcasters. 'Billie married Chris for richer and for poorer, and it looks like she got the latter,' is how one commentator saw it. The fact that Billie had already made plenty of money of her own seemed to pass people by – as did the fact that she was hardly a slave to designer shopping in the mould of a footballer's wife. Just after the court case, while spending a week at one of the most expensive hotels in the South of France, for example, Billie stunned fellow guests by heading down to the pool with her suntan cream, book, magazine and other necessities in a Spar carrier bag. You can take the girl out of Swindon, it seemed, but it appears that you really can't take Swindon out of the girl.

The French retreat would ultimately be notable for one other far more important factor than Billie's choice of summer bag, however. With Chris's court case over, the pair were ready to take some tentative steps into a new chapter of their lives. Their long, honeymoon-inspired career break was finally drawing to a close. Billie and Chris were both ready to get back to work, and they wanted to take on a series of entirely new professional challenges.

10
BILLIE PIPER:
SERIOUS ACTRESS

BILLIE'S NEW LIFE began under the warm Californian sun. She was getting used to the sky being blue when she woke in the mornings and she was desperately happy in her relaxed daily routine. She then climbed out of bed, padded around the house and on to the terrace where she looked out over LA towards the ocean. She went to get the papers and a coffee as usual and joined Chris beside their half-shaded pool. In theory, this day was just like any other day the couple spent in their Hollywood home. But Billie suddenly knew that it was different. She had made a decision; it was time to return to her childhood dreams. She wanted to see if she had what it took to be an actress.

'All our time travelling had been so liberating, I had had the time of my life. Chris wanted to escape as well.

We just wanted to have a great time together, to be rebels for a while. We did it for as long as we needed to do it. And then it was, "Right, we need to think about trying to do some work now." And we wanted to work because we felt completely inspired by what we had seen, what we had learned and the people we had met.'

Chris was totally supportive of his wife's sudden decision, just as she had known he would be. 'Back when we first met, it was Chris who said about my pop career, "You don't have to do this if you don't want to do it. It's your prerogative to take time out and get back into acting if that's what you really want to do." I took a while to see that and I couldn't have done it on my own. Sometimes, you are so involved that you can't see the wood for the trees. You need somebody to pick you up and shake you around to give you time to breathe.'

Now, nearly two years on, Billie felt it was time to learn. She realised, with a shock, that she had been away from Sylvia Young Theatre School for longer than she had actually been a student there. And in all her time away, she had had next to no time to consolidate any of the acting lessons she had taken as a girl. Once in a while, when filming a video perhaps, or when taking part in a sketch on kids' television, she had come close to inhabiting a new role and acting. But most of the time those skills had remained dormant and unacknowledged deep inside her. She needed to find out if she could dust them off and make them live again.

Fortunately, she didn't have much difficulty doing that.

She was in California, the entertainment capital of the world and, as Billie did some research, she felt that there sometimes seemed to be more acting schools than ordinary schools vying for students' custom. She decided she might as well learn from the very best, so she enrolled at the Larry Moss Studio.

Larry Moss was the man both Hilary Swank and Helen Hunt had thanked in their Best Actress Oscar acceptance speeches. His books on acting had been bestsellers and, when she walked into his classes, Billie was following the example of everyone from Jim Carrey, Leonardo DiCaprio and David Duchovny to Juliette Binoche, Christian Slater and Sally Field.

For Billie, the classes were rewarding on every level – boosting both her professional skills and her personal confidence. 'From the start, Los Angeles had been like a breath of fresh air because no one there knew who we were,' said Billie. 'With the acting lessons, this helped even more. I started classes and it was brilliant just to say, "I'm Billie from London," and make up the rest of my past. I never said I was a singer or anything like that because I just didn't want to sing any more. I needed to be anonymous. I wanted to approach acting school like any other student would.'

Billie thrived on the whole experience. 'I sharpened up what I had learned at Sylvia Young. There were classes in emotional memory. All the stuff that sometimes bordered on a crazy kind of therapy class. And outside of the classes, Chris and I were just left alone to do what we wanted without people staring at us. It couldn't have been nicer.'

After she and Chris headed back to Britain for a while, Billie felt she was ready for a new challenge. So when they got back to LA, she looked beyond the Larry Moss Studio in order to train under a different drama coach – Sabin Epstein. Her idea had simply been to expose herself to as many different lessons and points of view as possible to ensure she had the right foundations in place to forge her career as an actress. With Sabin, she took private lessons in his hideaway home a little deeper in the Hollywood Hills from her own house. And all the time she was looking ahead. The ambitious, focused, utterly well-prepared personality that Molly Tanner and David Calder had met at drama classes in Swindon, and that Sylvia Young had met in London, was back. And this time she brought a new sense of realism and self-awareness. 'I'm not a fool and I knew that being Billie Piper could get me through some doors as an actor,' she said candidly. 'But then I knew I would need to prove I was up for the job itself. That's why I wanted to go back to the lessons I had loved as a child. I wanted to make sure I was good enough.'

While Billie was taking her first steps back towards the world she had loved since childhood, Chris was heading straight back to the heart of British television. Their lives were in sync, just as they had been ever since they had first met. He had two high-profile shows on the go pretty much at the same time – the Vernon Kay-hosted *Boys and Girls* for Channel Four and *Live with Chris*

Moyles for Channel Five. Chris was the producer on both shows, although he also took the occasional cameo role in front of the cameras as well. Unfortunately for Chris, ratings never really took off for either show, and neither enjoyed many (if any) good reviews. The old Chris Evans magic didn't seem to be back when the Chris Moyles show was reinvented as *Live with Christian O'Connell*. What couldn't be denied, though, was Chris's pulling power as a producer – or his ability to bounce back from bad reviews.

So, next up, he got both Terry Wogan and Gaby Roslin on the same bill in a new Channel Five magazine slot, *The Terry & Gaby Show*. Danny Baker was on board as well and, once more, hopes were high. Again, though, the audience figures and the critical reactions were low and, after limping on for two long seasons, the show was taken off the air.

Making it back to the top of the entertainment world after a long, controversial and self-imposed exile wasn't proving as easy as Chris had hoped. And still in sync with her husband, Billie was facing just as many career challenges of her own. After flexing her acting muscles again in LA, she, too, was back in Britain looking for work. But for a whole host of reasons, this was proving very hard to find.

Experts said Billie's first and biggest problem was one of credibility. Her second was triggered by a form of envy. 'Billie had unwittingly fallen into the *Heat* and *Hello!* magazine world, famous for who she was, not for what she did,' says showbusiness reporter Laura Platt. 'She wanted to be taken seriously as an actress and, in truth, she had the stage school background to deserve that respect. But, in reality, people just didn't want to give it to her. For some sad reason, we all seemed to prefer seeing her as a talentless singer who had got lucky. She also fulfilled the country's need for an off-the-rails younger sister, someone whose car crash of a career made us feel better about our own failings. If she were to get that career back on track, if she were to succeed again, then did that mean we would have to sharpen up our acts as well? There was a palpable sense that we could all feel better about ourselves if Billie accepted the role we had given her, the role of the washed-up old has-been who had thrown it all away.'

The only problem, of course, was that Billie was working to a different script… and she was after a happy ending. So with her LA-found confidence intact, she began her latest re-invention. Billie the bubblegum pop star and Billie Piper the sultry R&B singer had both been ousted. Now she wanted the world to meet Billie Piper: Serious Actress. The only problem was that the world didn't seem to want to know.

Producers, directors, casting directors — everyone was brought into Billie's new charm offensive as she tried to meet as many people, shake as many hands and open as many doors as possible. She was sharing Chris's agent, Michael Foster, and she needed to get the message across that she was serious about returning to what had always been her vocation. But for all the polite interest that was expressed, her phone stubbornly refused to ring with offers of work. And on the rare occasion when she did get the chance to audition for a role, she says the baggage she seemed to be carrying made the process far tougher than she had ever imagined. 'When I was up for a job, I was very aware of thinking that some of these people know, or think they know, a great deal about my life. What underwear I wear, what time I fall out of pubs. I would walk into so many auditions feeling very vulnerable. There were moments of prejudice in terms of, "You're a pop star," and I could feel all the negativity around me. So I did some really shit auditions. The scripts were great, but I was shit.'

Less than five years earlier, at the height of her pop fame, Billie had given an interview when she had let slip that acting was still her real love, and that she one day hoped to star in a British film playing a psychopath or some other character quite different to herself. In 2002, as her list of failed auditions got ever longer, she would have been happy with almost any role going.

The one thing that Billie didn't do was give up. Fighting for what she wanted was in her DNA and, if she was losing on her current front, she decided to open up a new one elsewhere. After celebrating their second wedding anniversary, she and Chris sat at home and talked long into the night about how she could break through into the acting world. He couldn't have been more supportive. Earlier in the year, he had told friends how impressed he was by his wife's ability. 'Billie loves acting and is great on screen. I think she has found her niche. She is really talented,' he told them. Now he repeated it to Billie's face and tried to help her find ways to get that message across to others. They both agreed that Billie's own fears about being seen as a cartoon figure from the tabloids rather than as a serious actress were holding her back. They felt that casting directors' false impressions of her likely behaviour were doing the same. The pair had both read countless self-help books while out of the public eye and they distilled some of the most effective lessons from them into a new attitude and strategy for Billie.

'I had to stop myself from having a confidence crisis,' Billie said. 'I finally made a decision to stop inviting those negative kinds of thoughts, other people's preconceptions, into the auditions. I also wanted to make it clear that one thing I have never been is unprofessional. People used to say or think that I would turn up rolling drunk for filming and stuff and that was completely untrue and never going to happen. I would never do that and I had to get that message across.'

It could have been a coincidence or it could have been karma, but immediately after kicking out her mental demons, Billie won her first big break.

The rising star Orlando Bloom had picked up the lead role in a new British comedy *The Calcium Kid*. Billie had auditioned alongside several dozen other actresses for the part of his girlfriend, Angel, and says she gnawed her fingers almost to the bone waiting to hear if she had been picked. 'It was a small part but it was significant and it was perfect for me as it was my first film and I was nervous about finally making a breakthrough,' she says. 'I was terrified before, during and after the audition. I always am with things I care about. The adrenalin comes and I turn into this manic girl and have to force myself to stay calm.'

The role of Angel, as it was originally written, was particularly appealing to the occasionally world-weary Billie. 'She is a very pure and innocent character and I enjoyed the thought of taking that on,' she said. Billie also liked the calibre of the performers she met on set. Timothy Spall was cast in one of the main roles, alongside comic actress Ronni Ancona and new talent Omid Djalili. What Billie also liked was the unexpected sense of camaraderie she got when production finally began. Her life as a solo pop star had often been cripplingly lonely. Even her dancers on tour had normally been older than her and, because they had often worked together before, they enjoyed in-jokes and histories Billie couldn't share. She had often felt as if she were at the top of a very steep pyramid, with all the fun going on several layers beneath her.

On the set of *The Calcium Kid*, though, it was totally different. Everyone pitched in, nobody seemed to care how old anyone was, and Billie was in her element at the very middle of the pyramid. 'Suddenly, everyone you are working with is in your dreams every night,' she said of the intensity of her experience. 'It is a bubble, almost like *Big Brother*, where you all congregate for six weeks or however long it is and have to just get on and gel.'

And while the set itself was hardly the last word in Hollywood glamour (it was mostly filmed in gritty Kennington, south London, and up east on the Isle of Dogs), Billie says she felt at home on it from the very start. She got a sense of comfort and belonging that she had never fully experienced in the music industry. She was desperately hoping that this would be her first film set of many – but, for a long time, it looked as if this wish would never come true.

The film's producers were pitching *The Calcium Kid* squarely at the feel-good, zero-to-hero British comedy market that had been so lucratively colonised by the likes of *The Full Monty* and *Billy Elliot*. The plot was simple, charming and endearing. Orlando Bloom played the world's most cheerful milkman who accidentally injures Britain's big hope in the boxing World Championship. He is then the last man standing in the ring when a replacement contender has to be found. So can the milkman triumph in his bizarre new world? As stories go, the David versus Goliath tale is as old as the hills. But Billie and the other actors liked the comic 'mocumentary' style of the production and had high hopes that it could be the big summer hit.

As far as Billie was concerned, two things soon went wrong, however. The first was that almost all of her role ended up on the cutting-room floor as the editors tried to streamline the film's plot and keep its length under control. She didn't appear at all in the film's preview and what was left of her part involved strutting around in hot pants, thrusting her chest out at Orlando Bloom and smiling a lot. 'Billie Piper plays the most under-written love interest ever,' said one of the early reviewers. 'Her longest line is, "Can I have my knockers back, now?" and, yes, you really had to see it to know what that meant.'

The second problem for Billie, one shared with everyone else involved, was that the film wasn't ready for release in its first summer... and it didn't get released in the summer of 2003 either. The money men apparently wanted to wait until Orlando Bloom's star had risen as far as possible on the back of *The Lord of the Rings* before releasing *The Calcium Kid* to the cinemas. So no one would get the chance to see Billie's big screen breakthrough for quite some time.

When the film did come out, in the spring of 2004, it pretty much died on its feet (it didn't even get a release in any of the multiplexes in Billie's home town of Swindon). Reviewers were savage and it went straight to video in America. 'This is the film that Orlando Bloom will choose not to mention in future interviews and no doubt wishes would disappear altogether,' said no less a critic than the *Hollywood Reporter*. That said, Billie and Orlando had got on well together on set and there was talk of them starring together in a bigger-budget romantic comedy (which came to nothing) and in his next film *Kingdom of*

Heaven (in the event, the role earmarked for Billie went to another rising star, Eva Green).

So was Billie's new career on the skids, just as Chris's reincarnation as a television producer went through similar troubles? In tune with each other as ever, they decided to retreat for a few days while they planned their next moves – though, as usual, they did this in their own typical style. They checked into a health farm, the historic and stunningly beautiful Grayshott Hall in Surrey, to try and get their bodies and minds together. Billie was particularly hoping for some sort of divine inspiration from some of the spa's other famous guests – top actresses Judi Dench, Vanessa Redgrave, Joan Plowright and Maggie Smith had all been recent visitors. But while Billie and Chris both enjoyed several of the most relaxing treatments at the £200-a-night retreat, they did baulk at its 'no booze' rule. So no one was surprised to find them in the local village pub on their second night there, where Billie joined in a sing-a-long with some regulars.

Once more it seemed as if taking time out with her husband had given Billie the good vibes she needed to win more work. After getting back on the audition trail, she had another break. It was for television, rather than for a film. And it was an unusual project that was a gamble for everyone involved, but it turned out to be the role that would turn Billie's career around.

The show was a modern reworking of Chaucer's *The Canterbury Tales*, and it had an unusual beginning. In

2001, executive producer Laura Mackie had just been made Head of Drama Serials for the BBC and had been in Phoenix, Arizona, scouting out new locations for *Auf Wiedersehen Pet* with fellow producer Franc Roddam. 'We were looking for a new piece that reflected life in the new century. Franc mentioned *The Canterbury Tales* and what enduring stories they were. We discussed how it might be possible to update them to the present day and that sowed the seed of the idea.'

Two years later, the BBC was ready to give it a go. It had selected six tales for adaptation and picked a range of top contemporary writers to work on the scripts. The idea had been to film each one in intensive two- or three-week shoots, which the producers hoped would give them more chance of attracting top actors for the main roles. They were right – the likes of Julie Walters, James Nesbitt, Dennis Waterman and Jonny Lee Miller signed up. And Billie and her agent were certain that there was a dream role for her in Nesbitt and Waterman's show, *The Miller's Tale*.

The original story revolves around a devious lodger who tricks his landlord into believing a second biblical-scale flood is on the way. As the landlord sets about building tubs to save everyone from drowning, the lodger sets about seducing his young wife. Award-winning writer Peter Bowker was charged with adapting the story for today and his new version was set in a small-time karaoke pub in Kent. Dennis Waterman played the jealous, fifty-something pub owner keen to attract free-spending and desperately hopeful singers. James Nesbitt was Nick, a con artist who turned up and promised stardom to the publican's karaoke-loving young wife Alison.

It seemed a role Billie had been born to play. But Peter Bowker needed to be convinced. 'Casting the role was always going to be a bit of a dilemma. Do you cast a singer who can act or an actor who can sing?' he asked as the producers pulled together a list of possible Alisons. Billie, adrenalin flowing, feeling manic and having spent the morning gnawing away at her nails like a woman possessed, tried to look calm for her on-camera audition. *The Calcium Kid* seemed to be gathering dust on its distributor's shelves, so this show would be her chance finally to be respected as an actress and she was desperate to win it. She worked on her breathing, pushed aside her fears and gave it her all. It worked. Having been unsure whether to cast a top singer or a top actress, Peter Bowker was euphoric. 'With Billie we got both, and I think people will be very surprised by Billie Piper's acting,' he said.

'The camera loves Billie. I have seen it before, but never witnessed it so dramatically.' Having watched her audition and spoken to her at length afterwards, he was also taken aback by how easily she could shatter people's perceptions – including his own. 'People assume she will be some fluffy bunny who laughs in the right places and will be a bit vacuous. The other misconception is that she won't have a sense of humour about where she is and where she has come from. In *The Miller's Tale*, she was playing a singer, married to an older man, which might not seem like too much of a stretch. But, for all that, there was clearly proper acting going on. People came to me time and time again saying she blew them away in the role. Now, whenever I am in casting discussions, her name comes up.'

Laura Mackie was another very influential fan, saying Billie was 'a terrific new talent' while James Nesbitt was equally impressed. 'Billie is an original and has something which is a bit of a cliché – people call it star quality but it is a very rare aura and presence as a person. If you are lucky, then that transfers to the screen and it does so for Billie,' he said after the final scenes were filmed.

What Billie loved about the script was the chance to prove she had a sense of humour – something she was convinced a lot of people didn't see in her. So she revelled in the in-jokes, more than happy to play up to all the clever references to her professional past and personal present. And while she had secretly told herself that she didn't want to take on any roles that relied on her singing, she was more than happy to admit that filming some of the karaoke scenes had been a blast.

One other set of scenes would trigger even more attention, however, and, in filming them, Billie laid the 'sense of humour deficit' rumours to rest for good. The issue arose because *The Miller's Tale* is pretty much the bawdiest of *The Canterbury Tales*. English students say it includes one of the lewdest scenes in literature, when Alison and her suitor both poke their naked behinds out of a window for an admirer to kiss — a scene made even more enjoyable to schoolboy readers by the introduction of a red-hot poker and an unexpected fart. In for a penny, in for a pound, thought Billie towards the end of the three-week shoot, when the big scene was finally ready to be filmed. She dropped her skirt and gave her all — enjoying a stiff drink with cast and crew that evening as everyone toasted her ability to put embarrassment aside and get on with the job in hand.

Preview tapes of the series were released to the media in the late summer of 2003 and Arts commentator Bonnie Greer was an early fan of the original concept, of the individual productions and, most important of all, of Billie herself. 'The episodes I have seen so far — *The Knight's Tale*, *The Miller's Tale*, and *The Sea Captain's Tale* — are completely delightful,' Greer wrote in the *Mail on Sunday*. 'And, what's more, the series has produced a genuine star — Billie Piper.'

When Greer moved on to discuss the individual tales, Billie was in for even more praise. 'Everything about this tale is wonderful, especially Waterman and Nesbitt, two actors who could not give a bad performance at gunpoint,' wrote Greer. 'But it is Mrs Chris Evans who is the revelation. As Alison, the young wife, Piper lights up the screen to such an extent that you actually miss her when she is not there. Funny and heart-breaking at the same time, Piper sends up her own career as a singer with expert comic timing. Piper could be a serious cinematic contender,' she concluded.

For Billie, the sentiments could not have been better, and the praise was hugely important to her. In her time as a singer, she had ultimately grown able to dismiss her critics because her track record at the top of the charts had meant she knew that she had already proved herself. If some record reviewers had said she was no good, it didn't matter, because the industry insiders and the fans knew otherwise. Starting out in her new profession, Billie had no such safety net to fall back on. Bad reviews so early in her new world could push her right off the wire and give her very little chance of climbing back up again.

In London, another important person had been watching *The Miller's Tale* with particular interest. Sylvia Young wanted to see whether her former pupil had lost her spark as an actress after so long in the music world and the celebrity wilderness. She was euphoric to find that Billie was as good as she had remembered. 'From the moment Billie stepped into our school for her first audition, I knew there was something special about her,' Sylvia told reporters. 'We always knew her real talent lay in acting. She only ever got into the singing world by mistake. It was obvious she would be brilliant in pop but she is also a fine, fine actress who can do anything from soaps to Shakespeare. Billie was without doubt of National Theatre quality.'

Sylvia also had the evidence to back this up. Full reports are kept on every Sylvia Young pupil and Billie's were among the best Sylvia had seen. 'Sitting here looking through Billie's file, every report from every teacher said she was brilliant. When she was 13, one of our drama coaches described her as "very talented, indeed potentially brilliant". He went on to say that she had an incredible comic talent as well, and this is one of the hardest kinds of acting.'

As if this vote of confidence wasn't enough, even better news came when *The Canterbury Tales* was finally broadcast and the audience figures were released. Amazingly, for a high-risk show which could easily have turned off a mass audience, *The Miller's Tale* attracted just under 8 million viewers — not quite up there with an average night on *EastEnders*, but more than almost everyone connected to the project had dared to hope for. Billie Piper the actress felt she had enjoyed the best possible launch. She was in the mainstream, and she had just fought tooth and nail to win another even more challenging role that she was hoping would keep her there.

The Bafta award-winning documentary director Brian Hill was the man she needed to impress to get her second big job of the year. He had been commissioned by the BBC to make a drama for a series it was planning, examining the lives of people in care. The programme was to be called *Bella and the Boys*. It had a complex structure and plot, largely told through flashbacks, and whoever took the title role would have two jobs to do. First, she would have to shine as the loud, mouthy teenager up for a good time and sex in the back of a stolen car, and then as the subdued single-mother whose life has taken one too many hard knocks. It meant casting was tough. 'Obviously, I needed someone who could play a 15-year-old and a 28-year-old and I saw between 25 and 30 actors for the role,' says Brian.

One of those dozens of hopeful actresses was Billie, and Brian admits she had obstacles to overcome from the moment she walked into her first audition. Fortunately, she immediately proved she could overcome them. 'Billie certainly wasn't as experienced as some of the other people we saw, but she had an enthusiasm and an understanding that I was looking for, certainly when it came to the 15-year-old. In the end, I thought she had something special. There's a steeliness and strength to her that was very important in the part.'

When her agent got the call saying the part was hers, Billie was euphoric, not least because she knew this role would stretch her as an actress. As it turned out, the job would affect her personally as well. Much of the intense three-week shoot was physically and emotionally tough, not least because much of the action was filmed in real care homes amidst genuine residents. 'Until you spend time in places like that, you are kind of blind and deaf to some of the things that people go through in life. You read about them in the papers but you never really get inside the person's head, and so working with these kids that had such crappy starts in life made me think a lot and made it a great project to work on,' Billie said afterwards. 'Even though Bella is surrounded by people of her own age, she is a very lonely character. As I had left home at 12 and been without my family when I had been on tour as a singer, I had been lonely as well. I tapped into the memories of my own loneliness at that time to play Bella.'

Wherever her inspiration came from, it showed up on Billie's face on screen. The drama got nothing like the ratings or the reviews of *The Miller's Tale*, but the comments that were made were almost wholly positive. Billie felt, finally, that she was on her way. At last she had a real CV as an actress, and it felt fantastic. 'I finally feel at home in my career, I don't feel like an alien when I'm acting,' she told reporters back in Swindon. 'Playing Bella is the most challenging piece of work I have done and it is one I feel really satisfied with.'

What she was also proud about was her ability to rise above the long-standing fears and insecurities which had sprung up again now she was back at work. 'I don't bite my nails or smoke unless I'm working,' she admitted, looking back with a trace of regret about the lazy calmness of her sabbatical period. 'When I'm working, I put pressure on myself and make it more panicky than it should be.'

The girl who had turned into an insomniac worrying about her pop performances was trying desperately not to fall into the same pattern as an adult. But at first this wasn't easy, because in some ways being in front of the cameras was even more stressful than being in front of a microphone at a concert. As a teenage extra on her first two films, *Evita* and *The Leading Man*, she had been in awe of the sheer numbers of people hanging around on film sets. Now she was out of the crowd scenes and needing to carry a shot on her own, she was feeling the pressure. 'You don't realise the responsibility of filming until you are on the set, surrounded by crew and everyone is waiting for you to say a line and get it right,' she said of her new life in the spotlight.

After *Bella and the Boys* had been made and broadcast, other insecurities were also bubbling just below Billie's surface. After one film and two BBC shows, she had allowed herself to relax just a little bit about her prospects. In typical fashion, this was just when the work seemed to dry up. Billie was doing the rounds with a huge number of auditions, and she was about to face a hefty round of knock-backs.

First of all, she failed to win the role she wanted in the Richard Eyre film *Stage Beauty* (an adaptation of the stage play *Compleat Female Stage Beauty*). This meant missing out on the chance to work with Rupert Everett, Tom Wilkinson, Ben Chaplin and Billy Crudup – the role Billie had hoped for ended up going to Claire Danes. She lost the big role as Jude Law's girlfriend in *Alfie* to Sienna Miller, and got nowhere in her bid for a part in the big-screen superhero film *Fantastic Four*. Then there was the role of Nancy in Roman Polanski's *Oliver Twist* – a role Billie was desperate for and convinced she had been born to play. It went to another rising star, Leanne Rowe, and Billie said she was 'so gutted' she could hardly speak for a day after finding she had missed out.

The workaholic in Billie meant that while she was auditioning for and missing out on these major film roles, she wasn't ignoring any other opportunities either. Unfortunately, these all seemed to end with the same rejections. She was turned down for each of the roles of presenter, choreographer and judge that she had been considered for on *Popstars: The Rivals*, and missed out on the role she had wanted in the new, much delayed West End production of Noel Coward's *Hay Fever*.

As rejection piled upon rejection, even the individual moments at auditions seemed to go awry. Then there was the day when her character had to hold a six-month old baby – something she hadn't a lot of experience of in real life. 'The director just yelled out, "Billie, we're going to have to do that again because you look so awkward." It was embarrassing,' Billie admits. And once more she didn't get the job.

But not for nothing had agent Michael Foster called his client one of the most ambitious people he had met in 25 years in the entertainment industry; Billie was also one of the most determined. She vowed to brush aside every knock back, every rejection, every refusal. She would pay her dues as an actress like all the other struggling professionals she saw at auditions. Then, if success finally came, it would seem all the sweeter.

What Billie was also finding was just how slow-burn an acting career can be. So many people get labelled overnight sensations in the industry. But, most of the time, they had been plugging away unseen for years before suddenly getting a break. Just as frustrating was the huge time-lag between playing a part and seeing it on screen. For experienced stars, this didn't really matter, because their past body of work can support them through any delays. But Billie, as usual, was in a hurry. When she had played a role, she wanted it seen. But her next two jobs would test her patience to the limit.

The first delay came after she won the role of Vicky in a new British comedy drama that was very much in the genre of *The Calcium Kid*. And just like that film, there was precious little Hollywood glamour. *Things to Do Before You're 30* was made in London and the Isle of Man with a £3 million budget and a strong cast of young actors. It followed the typically messy lives of a group of 20-something friends struggling to come to terms with adulthood.

As usual, Billie had high hopes that her role would get her noticed – not least because she played the flirty new girlfriend who shared a full-blown kiss with actress Keira Jane Malik in a pivotal 'threesome' scene. When the film's original publicity was devised, Billie's status as a film newcomer left her feeling like an after-thought, however. '*Things to Do Before You're 30* – starring Dougray Scott (*Mission Impossible: 2, Ripley's Game*), Jimi Mistry (*The Guru*), Emilia Fox (*The Pianist*), Shaun Parkes (*The Mummy Returns, Human Traffic*) and Billie Piper,' was how the film was first presented to the media in 2004. As it turned out, Billie would edge up the billing before the film finally hit the cinemas. It was released in Europe and some other parts of the world in late 2005 and, by the time British cinema audiences saw it in the summer of 2006, Billie was a bona fide star.

Funnily enough, she would start that leap up the career ladder while on the set of her next film — even though this would end up providing her with some of the worst reviews of her life.

The film was *Spirit Trap*, directed by advertising wonder-boy David Smith. The plot centred on a group of students in a spooky mansion in London and the film was trying to tap into the renewed success of the horror film genre, with such movies as *Scream*, *I Know What You Did Last Summer* and *Scary Movie*. *Spirit Trap* wanted to be the next big hit and Billie was excited to be part of it. 'I made it partly because I love horror films. When I was younger, too young to go out on the lash, I would watch horror films and scare myself out of my wits instead. So when the opportunity came to do my own one, I could hardly resist it,' she said.

But the film was no easy ride. After a week of rehearsals, where the cast members were encouraged to improvise, re-work and even re-write the script, they flew to Romania for an intense 27-day shoot. 'We had a fantastic cast but we were working on a very tight schedule, we worked extremely hard and we had to get everything right first time,' said David. He said Billie, playing the lead role, was a tower of strength throughout the shoot, putting up with all the unexpected difficulties and delays of filming in cheap and not always efficient locations.

'Her acting ability is extraordinary,' he said when the cast were back in Britain for four final days of much smoother London-based shoots. But the film itself was already rumoured to be running into trouble. It took time before it was released and, for a while, it looked as if it might not make it into the cinemas at all. Billie, who was up front and centre in the film posters, bore the brunt of the bad reviews when it finally opened. 'Most of the acting is astonishingly inept and Billie Piper simply passes on valuable information to the other characters in the same flat voice that others might use to read out fire regulations. Her accent wanders from Roedean to Romford and she acts throughout as though recently stunned by falling masonry,' said the *Daily Mail*'s review. 'The film is horrific, but not in the way that the director intended,' wrote website Film 247.

Making matters worse was the rumour that, by the time the film was released in August 2005, the post-*Doctor Who* Billie was too big for her boots and had refused to help promote it. She admitted that she hadn't perhaps given her best performance on screen but was desperately upset by the claims that she was letting anyone down after the event. 'The tabloid nonsense about me not supporting the film has upset a lot of good friends I made on that film. I had a lot of fun filming it and, as an actor, you want to work and you learn so much more from being on a film set than you do in drama school, so this was really insightful for me. It was educational and I don't regret it at all. The way I look at it is this – sometimes you do bad things and sometimes you do good things. Sometimes people respond well to your work, and sometimes they don't. But when opportunity comes along in this business, you have to take it. You learn from it and you grow.'

Critical reaction aside, Billie knew that *Spirit Trap* would always have a special place in her memory. That was because her mobile phone had gone off during the very first script meeting on the set in Romania. The call was from her agent, and he had good news to pass on about *Doctor Who*.

11
THE DOCTOR'S ASSISTANT

BILLIE WASN'T WILDLY excited when her agent first told her that the BBC was rumoured to be planning a big-budget revival of *Doctor Who*; it wasn't a show she had really grown up with. Older kids at school sometimes talked about it and she knew her parents had enjoyed it but, apart from that, she had had no connection with it. 'It had been on in the background at home but, to me, it was like an old song the adults dance to at family weddings,' she said. 'Something you somehow know the words to but wouldn't choose to play on your own.'

She had two other reservations about the project when she first heard about it. She knew full well that, when it came to work, beggars can't be choosers, and she didn't want to think that any possible job was beneath her. But a tiny bit of her had preferred the grown-up, experimental nature of *The Miller's Tale* and *Bella and the*

Boys. Doctor Who, in comparison, seemed a little childish and mainstream for her tastes.

Still, always preferring to work if at all possible, Billie told Michael to keep her posted and, in the meantime, she had plenty to occupy her mind. The biggest challenge came on the home front. Out of nowhere, a Russian billionaire had just made the kind of financial offer you don't refuse for Hascombe Court in Surrey – so after nearly three happy years there as a married couple, Chris and Billie were preparing to sell up and move out. Fortunately, the potential upheaval of the change was tempered by the fact that, in the first instance, they weren't moving far. They had decided to live in a four-bedroom 'cottage' in their old home's grounds so they wouldn't lose touch with their friends in the local community. This new house, weirdly enough, directly overlooked the swimming pool at their old one, so they could enjoy the view of it while no longer being able to dip in it on summer's evenings.

Downsizing, though, was likely to be just a temporary measure. Billie was getting ready for her trip to Romania to film *Spirit Trap* and planned to join Chris for some real house-hunting on her return. But, before then, she had been told a lot more about *Doctor Who*, and the more she learned, the more she wanted to be part of it. What swung things for Billie was the news that *Queer as Folk* and *Second Coming* writer Russell T Davies was the driving force behind the project and would be writing the majority of its first set of scripts. His ground-breaking, grown-up style, his reputation for pushing artistic boundaries and his passion for making a new and iconic *Doctor Who*, suggested this would be no ordinary television revival.

Information was also leaking out about the huge amount of money the BBC was putting behind the series, about the other top writers being signed up – including *The League of Gentlemen*'s Mark Gatiss and *Coupling*'s Steven Moffatt – and about the possibility that 'actor's actor' Christopher Eccleston was up for the title role. Suddenly, the new *Doctor Who* was looking like the mainstream television show of the year. It wasn't long, therefore, before Billie became very, very keen to be on board.

With so much hype building up about the show, it was little wonder that Billie wasn't alone in expressing interest in the assistant's role. But it turned out that Russell T Davies would need plenty of persuading about her suitability. 'All I really had was the "celeb" impression of Billie that you get from magazines like *Heat*,' had said. He had no firm opinion on her ability as an actress or about her reliability as a person, and he had plenty of other people in mind for the role. 'It was pretty close to the kind of search they had to do to find Scarlett O'Hara,' he says of the audition process. 'We cast our net wide seeing some wonderful new talent as well as some rising stars. Everyone coming through our door had something exciting to offer and many of them could have done a superb job in the role.' But the final four dozen hopeful names were ultimately whittled down to those of just six actresses – one of whom was Billie Piper.

She says her biggest challenge in the early auditions was to try and keep her performances from following any pre-set pattern. 'I didn't watch loads of *Doctor Who* DVDs before my auditions. I went in with a fresh eye because I felt they wanted a fresh approach rather than a copy of something which everyone saw ten or twenty years earlier. I felt the whole point of the character is that she lives in today's world so that was the character I wanted to bring into the room.'

But would the production team agree? The selection process was about to move up a gear and get even tougher. Unbeknownst to the hopeful actresses, Christopher Eccleston had been confirmed in his role as the ninth *Doctor Who* and he was going to have an integral part in the casing of his assistant. 'We invited six actors back to read some scenes, on camera, with Christopher,' says Russell. 'They were six great readings and we only wished there were six companions for the Doctor.' But he says Billie was the only one of the hopeful actresses who really made the hairs stand up on the back of his neck as he watched her. As far as Russell was concerned, the auditions were now closed – and fortunately everyone else in the production team agreed with him. 'Billie was perfect. She was shining and clever and independent – just like the Rose I have had in my head. We all agreed after the final readings that Billie was the one, as did all our bosses. The final stage of the process was when our executive producer Julie Gardner and I met with Billie to talk her through the whole of Rose's story. Auditions don't allow enough time to explain everything, so this was our chance to tell Billie about every stage of Rose's journey – her hopes and ambitions and the terrible things waiting for her in outer space. Rose Tyler then came to life in front of us and we couldn't have been happier.'

Billie had flown off to Romania with the *Spirit Trap* crew while the BBC executives put contracts together for her. The call she took on her first day overseas was official confirmation that she had got the job – though she was sworn to secrecy until the corporation itself made the big announcement.

That came on Monday, 24 May. Billie Piper was indeed to be Rose Tyler in the forthcoming show. 'Doctor Who has his new assistant! Billie is beautiful, funny and intelligent. We needed to find a unique, dynamic partner for Christopher Eccleston and Billie fits the bill perfectly,' said producer Julie Gardner as she announced the news.

She and the other producers explained the basic premise that would kick off the new series: that the Doctor arrives on earth and meets an energetic, inquisitive, excited, optimistic, worldly yet naïve human being. Put like that, it was obvious why it had to be Billie, as she herself was more than happy to explain when she came back to Britain with one more film under her belt.

'I took the part because I could relate to Rose and I

knew I was very similar. As a child, I realised that I wanted something to happen in life, I wanted a bit more than I had. I wanted to find someone or something to challenge my ideas and broaden my horizons, so I definitely tapped into that part of Rose. It's that feeling of wanting something to happen and not knowing how to go about it. I felt that when I was in Swindon at the age of 14 and I wanted to get out. Rose is the same. It just takes a 900-year-old man in a blue box to get her going. I don't know if it is life imitating art or art imitating life, but I have led quite a strange and fascinating life for seven or eight years, so being on *Doctor Who* seems made-to-measure. I can definitely relate to that feeling of being trapped and wanting to go out there and to see more of the world and what it has to offer.'

However hard it was to argue with comments like this, it was soon clear that many people were unhappy about the BBC's decision. 'Christopher Eccleston is a great choice for the Doctor, but Billie Piper? Come on! If the BBC wants to kill the series before it's started, they are going about it the right way. What next? Dale Winton as the Master? Esther Rantzen as Davros? Let's just go the whole hog and have the cast of *Holby City* sprayed silver and use them as Cybermen. Why does the BBC think *Doctor Who* has to become light entertainment?' wrote one die-hard fan in *Doctor Who* magazine.

Others were equally damning and plenty of grossly offensive comments about Billie's ability and the way she had supposedly won the job started to be posted on

Internet message boards and in chat rooms. Bear in mind the fact that the show's production staff would soon be receiving hate mail over everything from the show's new logo and updated theme tune to the size of the TARDIS windows, and you can see how sensitively any changes to the show have to be treated. Apart from occasional repeats and the American-funded big screen adventure with Paul McGann in 1996 (dubbed 'Who Goes to Hollywood' by the critics), the series hadn't been on television since 1989. A whole generation had grown up without the show, and several generations had had plenty of time to wrap their memories of it up in an extraordinary mystique which would put huge pressure on anyone trying to recreate the early magic.

Fortunately, Billie did win over some influential supporters. *Doctor Who* magazine's assistant editor, Tom Spilsbury, was one of them. 'For some reason, probably due to the froth like *I'm a Celebrity, Get Me on the Telly*, there remains an unfair perception that the darlings of *Heat* magazine have little talent beyond being famous and there have already been rumblings among a minority of fans that Billie's casting is a grave mistake if *Doctor Who* is to be taken "seriously" by the viewing public. What utter nonsense,' he wrote when he was given the chance to put his personal opinions in his magazine. 'Shame on all the critics. If anything, Billie's casting is positive proof of just how seriously everyone on the new production team is taking their job. Billie, you're in for one hell of an adventure,' he concluded.

Halfway through the filming schedule, Russell T Davies would admit that he had been well aware of the potential downsides of casting such a tabloid-friendly figure as Billie in such an important television role. But he said his worries had been proved groundless, first at the audition stage and then on every day of filming that was to come. 'The unspoken deal in my head was that Billie can be in as many papers as she likes but we can't be stuck with a bad actor for 13 weeks. I had to be sure she would be committed to the role and show the level of determination you would expect from a top actor. I got that message straight away... and she has been magnificent. Very, very excellent. What people forget is that this is a drama, not light entertainment. Casting Chris and then Billie was a double whammy. Sometimes I still can't believe we pulled it off because it single-handedly changed the show's image and pushed us in the direction we wanted to go.'

For her part, Billie soon found out that she was taking something of a career gamble with the role. Fans of the series were quick to point out that the Doctor's assistants don't always stay in the job for long – since 1963, there have been nearly 20 assistants playing alongside less than half as many Doctors. Many of the actresses, including Bonnie Langford and *Bergerac* to *EastEnders* star Louise Jameson say the role was a joy from start to finish. But a worrying proportion of the other former assistants tell a different story.

'The role was a curse,' said Carole Ann Ford, who

played the first assistant, Susan Foreman, nearly half-a-century earlier. 'After Susan, I only ever got offered parts as kookie girls.' Janet Fielding, who played Tegan Jovanka between 1981 and 1984, said the role was 'the kiss of death' to her acting career. And one other former assistant, Anneke Willis, who played Polly with Doctors William Hartnell and Patrick Troughton between 1966 and 1967, had an even more profound warning to give. She said that when she saw Billie on screen, it was like seeing her own younger self — and the feeling of recognition only got stronger when she learned about the younger actress's life.

Just like Billie, Anneke had been picked for the role because the producers said she was a classic example of her era. 'I was the first sexy assistant. I was a classic dolly bird with eyelashes longer than my skirts,' says Anneke with a smile. She, just like Billie, had been a drama student who scandalised the press with her love life and had been a staple of the gossip columns of her day. Also, just like Billie, Anneke had ultimately married a man nearly twice her age. Where Anneke hoped their stories would differ would be in what happened next. After a wonderful time in the TARDIS, Anneke's extraordinary journey would take in drugs, rock 'n' roll, a cult, a commune, tragic deaths, new starts and endless financial, personal and health setbacks. When Billie took on the assistant's role, Anneke was living like a hermit in a tiny rented cottage on the edge of Dartmoor. She was happy and at peace with the world, but she hoped the woman she recognised from her television screen would learn from her mistakes and follow a smoother path. 'I would say to Billie, "Life is never as straightforward as you think it is going to be,"' Anneke said when asked to give the Doctor's latest assistant some advice. Unfortunately for Billie, she was about to be proved right.

The filming schedule for *Doctor Who* meant that, for the next eight months, Billie would spend a minimum of eleven days every fortnight in Cardiff. Most of the series was filmed in a vast studio complex just outside Newport, in south Wales, and on location around the country. For the foreseeable future, life for Billie was to be centred around a rented apartment or a hotel room, with Chris planning to head down the M4 to visit as often as he could.

From the start, *Doctor Who* was big news for the Cardiff area. A lot of existing jobs at BBC Wales were secured on the back of the show, and even more new ones were created. The buzz that built up around the show was equally important to the local economy, even though it sometimes got so loud that it threatened to put the whole production off schedule.

On the very first day of filming, for example, Cardiff City Council accidentally leaked details of where the initial scenes were being shot. So as well as huge numbers of fans, some 60 paparazzi photographers were prowling around the area, most of them wanting shots of Billie. 'I was terrified it would throw her, but she just ignored it and got on with her job. I was amazed and impressed by that and it showed just how much inner strength she has,' said Russell T Davies, who had feared the leak would force them to waste valuable days of film time.

In the end, the team got some useable footage on their very first day, and Billie and Christopher Eccleston discovered they were going to be good friends. 'I think we were well cast from the beginning. Very cleverly put together,' said Christopher. 'And we had a great time, even though it was very hard work. We didn't know each other at all when we started and we were immediately together for eight months, six days a week, 14 to 15 hours a day, both with our careers on the line, hers at the beginning, mine in the middle. I think we did really well. The Doctor has always been a hero, but there has never been a heroine out there for 8-to-12 year-old girls and women. Well, now there is. Billie carries the series with me. We do it together, a man and a woman. There are huge emotional episodes in the series and Billie pulled them off.'

The pair became regulars at Cardiff's cool Salt Bar and also left the city for dinners in country pubs on the rare occasions when their filming schedules allowed.

For a while, there was all the usual tabloid gossip that the pair might be more than just friends and colleagues. But, as it turned out, they had a very good reason for spending so much time together: Billie was lonely because her husband was no longer visiting as often as they had hoped. In the middle of the biggest job of her career, it seemed as if her marriage might well be over.

And, as had happened all her life, the crisis would be played out in the full glare of national publicity.

12
GOODBYE, CHRIS

PACKING HER BAGS to leave for the start of filming in Cardiff had been a big deal for Billie – and for Chris. She knew she was going to be away every weekday and most weekends for the next eight months. It was the kind of enforced separation which would have put pressure on even the most ordinary, relaxed and flexible of marriages. But, for Billie and Chris, the development meant even more. This would be so different to the way that they had lived their lives to date that it could hardly fail to cause problems. 'We had been completely inseparable until this point. Since we met, we had been together pretty much 24 hours a day, 7 days a week and it had worked. This was the first time we had really been apart and it had made us both think about things,' Billie said, falteringly, when asked about their sudden change of circumstances.

At first, however, they had high hopes of riding out any separation storms. Chris was throwing himself into his new stable of television shows, including a planned new series staring Johnny Vegas. But he aimed to keep as many weekends free as possible to visit his wife in Wales, and she wanted to head back to Surrey or London to see him whenever she had a break as well. What gave them so much confidence about their futures was the fact that Chris was genuinely proud of his wife's achievements as an actress, while she was fiercely supportive of his return to television production. Neither of them had ever had any trouble finding things to talk about — and now they had been given a huge new range of interests and experiences to discuss.

Billie, in particular, had plenty to say during that first summer in Wales. She needed a lot of reassurance from Chris about how she was doing on set, and the sheer scope and size of the show meant there was always some new anecdote to discuss when she was in her hotel room with Chris at the end of another long day.

The problem was that, as the weeks turned into months, she was increasingly tired — and the *Doctor Who* schedule meant she was working even more days than she had first thought. Chris was left to wait around for her on the days they had thought were going to be free. Billie also had fewer chances to leave Wales and visit him back at home, and both realised that something fundamental had changed in their relationship. If that change had not felt so serious, then there would always have been a chance that they could have patched things up until the filming ended and they were back living in the same house again. But both knew that if *Doctor Who* took off, Billie would be back in Wales for another gruelling eight-month stint the following year. And even if the show wasn't re-commissioned, she would no doubt be winning other jobs with equally tough schedules elsewhere.

Some couples say having plenty of space keeps their love alive. Marriage counsellors say work-related separations can sometimes help a couple by making their reconciliations all the sweeter. But Billie and Chris both knew that this kind of life wasn't for them. They had proved it in 2001 by getting married within six months of their first proper date and then spending almost every subsequent night together. As far as they were concerned, marriage was a full-time, all-or-nothing business. This new life wasn't what they had signed up to... and they could no longer hide the truth.

'It all just felt a bit weird,' Billie says of the turning point weekend in Wales when Chris had been visiting and they both realised things were going wrong. 'I remember Chris just saying what I was thinking. He said something like, "I don't know if this is working out and I don't want to stop you or hold you back." I think it was then we knew it was over,' Billie says softly.

'I still love Billie. We're going to divorce.' With those eight words, Chris publicly confirmed the split that had been gossiped about in the tabloids for several months. It was the early autumn and he was talking to *News of the*

World reporter Rav Singh, a man who had known both stars before their marriage and had become a close confidant of theirs shortly afterwards. 'They were two sentences that simply don't belong together,' Rav said, clearly upset for a man he saw as a friend. And Chris was to hold plenty more sad conversations as official news of the split finally started to spread. 'I thought we were going to be together for ever. We were going to grow old together but, somewhere along the way, it just didn't happen and it is very painful,' was how he described his feelings after the split. 'No one could have predicted how Billie's career was going to take off. None of us knew she would turn out to be this amazing actress. But I knew that if we stayed married, I would hold her back and I didn't want to. Geography is very important in a marriage. It is never going to work if you are in separate places doing separate things. But more than that, I knew how important it was for her to go off and do her thing. If we were married, I would have wanted her to be with me and you just can't do that to someone. I want her to be happy and I want her to do well. Although splitting up has hurt, it was the best thing we ever did... apart from marrying in the first place.'

It was clear from the moment the split was confirmed that Billie and Chris were never going to get involved in a public blame game. Neither, it appeared, were they ever going to speak ill of each other. What had happened was desperately sad, but no extra energy was to be wasted on recriminations.

'We have gone our separate ways as husband and wife, but we are still very much part of each other's lives and always will be. Chris is the most amazing person that I have ever met. I could never not have him in my life. First and foremost, he is and will remain my best friend,' was how Billie described the situation when the clamour for her side of the story grew too intense to ignore. So why had they split, after defying the critics and seeming to be so happy for so long? 'Our relationship just ran its natural course,' she said softly. 'We just wanted to do different things in the end; it is really that simple. And it is sad, but we are just getting on with it. We shared something special and unique. He saved me from a lot and helped me so much with my life and I hope I helped him as well. I will for ever be grateful to him for that. Our split has not been as tough as everyone thinks. It's all very friendly, there are no bad feelings or resentment. It is very amicable.'

But why now? Is there someone else? Did one of you cheat? Is it about money? Has your whole relationship up until now been a sham? The questions, for both Billie and Chris, were being asked every time they left their front doors. And many of them were, frankly, bizarre.

As she tried to fend them off, Billie found herself forced to step back three years in time and explain yet again why she had married Chris in the first place – a clear irony for an actress whose day job put her in a time machine. Billie was particularly angry that their original motives for marrying were suddenly under scrutiny again. 'The relationship worked for me and it worked for him and we were both really, really happy. Do I regret it? No. Would I do it all again? Yes. Am I proud of the time we spent together? More than anything.'

Chris said almost exactly the same thing when quizzed by Michael Parkinson after the split. 'You know, our relationship was only for three years, but I would happily have thirty of those three years all over again,' he said.

As the questions and interview requests mounted up, Billie was also quizzed about the pressures that had triggered the separation. Chris's ex-wife Carol McGiffin was tracked down by reporters for her thoughts on the matter, and she said she thought the marriage was doomed from the moment Billie had asserted her own independence as a professional and successful actress. The implication was that if Billie had remained at home to stroke her husband's ego, join him on his drinking binges and wait around for him while he played golf with his older friends, then the marriage would have survived.

When it came to the Evans marriage, the newspaper columnists decided that *Doctor Who* had an awful lot to answer for. It was a theory Billie shot down as soon as she heard it. 'I don't blame the job. I think whatever happened between Chris and me would have happened in the end anyway. I would never ever say the job was responsible for my divorce because that would be stupid. Chris and I had a great time while we were together and that's all that concerns me. We are best buddies and we always will be.'

As for the future, the pair were determined not to jeopardise this extraordinary friendship. By November, their split was official and complete, but they decided that they would wait two years before divorcing, so they could end their marriage without either side having to blame the other for the collapse. It was a final, civilised touch to a very public but strangely dignified split, one that was sealed in the autumn of 2006.

Suddenly single, Billie had two people she could rely on absolutely for support – her parents. Almost a decade ago, Mandy had said the first rule of parenting was to accept that you might not see much of your children when their lives are going well, but that you have to be ready to help them if the tide ever turns. Today, with her eldest daughter all grown up, she was ready to prove it. The estrangement that had built up after Billie left home and became a teenager at stage school had been bridged, and the hurt Mandy had felt after being excluded from Billie's wedding day had long since been forgotten. So, as the media storm raged, she and Paul were on their way to Wales to tell their daughter that they loved her.

'My mum and dad are there for me. There is none of that "I told you so" or being disapproving and wagging fingers. They are just my mates and that is what I need now,' Billie said. Everyone also agreed that what Billie also needed was a distraction – and *Doctor Who* was ready to provide it. She had carried on working every day while her marriage was disintegrating. She had worked on while the press demanded as many details they could get about the split — and made up any that were off limits to them. And she says that this single-minded focus saw her through the worst times. The work ethic she had inherited from her father would end up saving her. 'I was in a bubble, pretty much oblivious to everything going on outside *Doctor Who*. I threw myself into my work 100 per cent and that helped me cope with it all,' she says. And there was a huge amount of work to do.

By the time Billie was officially on her own again, she and the rest of the *Doctor Who* crew were working on some pretty high-profile scripts and with some seriously A-list actors. As well as Russell T Davies, Mike Gatiss and Steven Moffat, the first series also had contributions from award-winning *Coronation Street* writer Paul Cornell. The cast had included cameo roles from the likes of Simon Callow, Simon Pegg and Penelope Wilton. In December, five months into the eight-month filming schedule, another new face joined the gang — the actor and singer John Barrowman, who was coming into the TARDIS as Captain Jack. He and Billie had a complicated romantic scene together on their first day on set, and they got on like a house on fire from the start.

'Apart from anything else, I think it was fun for Billie to have someone new around because filming had been very long and very intense up until then,' he says, very aware that the post-split Billie might be feeling vulnerable and alone. 'Everyone was tired on the set, but the atmosphere was still good. We were excited about what we were creating and everyone was starting to get nervous about how it might be received.'

What particularly lifted Billie's spirits was the fact that the overall tone of the completed episodes were perfectly in tune with her own personality and life goals. When she had first been told about the series, she had been concerned about playing a peripheral, dolly-bird character whose chief role was to be patronised by an all-knowing Doctor. She needn't have worried. In this 21st-century incarnation, equality ruled. Rose Tyler was to be central to every part of the action – and, for the first time, she would bring real sexual tension to the TARDIS. The interaction between the Doctor and Rose would be central to the show's success, but it was left deliberately hard to define.

'It's a relationship you can't put your finger on,' says Billie. 'There's a lot of holding hands. It's however you choose to perceive it. There has never been a relationship like this between the Doctor and his assistant before. In the past, the other doctors have been slightly chauvinistic and patronising to their assistants. But, in this case, they are on a par. Rose teaches him stuff he is not quite familiar with and vice-versa. They show each other their worlds and they share them; they're a perfect team. I love the sci-fi of the show, but the thing that really got me going was the relationship stuff. I love the concept of this man walking into this girl's life and turning it on its head for her.'

In so many ways, and with a huge hint of sadness, it

could have been Chris Evans rather than Christopher Eccleston she was talking about.

Billie also admitted to friends that while she loved the high-tech nature of the show when it was all on the screen, the challenge of actually filming it was another matter entirely. This new big-budget *Doctor Who* was determined to stamp out the fabled wobbly sets and *Blue Peter*-style monsters of the past. A huge amount of the show's budget was to go on special effects and vast teams of CGI workers were employed to put together the kind of scenes that matched the best from Hollywood. So in a single episode, you could see alien spacecraft hurtling across the London skyline, clipping Big Ben and crashing into the Thames.

Much of the work was done by The Mill, the team responsible for the Oscar-winning film *Gladiator*, who were told to give the show the strongest possible look. 'I hope everyone, adults and children, watches it from behind the sofa,' said special-effects supremo Will Cohen. And as the plot lines got darker (raising plenty of comment from worried parents), that certainly looked as if it might be the case.

Being the actor in the middle of all this computer-generated mayhem wasn't always easy, however. There could be a vast amount of sitting around while even the shortest of scenes were set up. Many of the scenes were filmed blind, with all the action added later. And everyone knew that if they messed up, it could cost a huge amount of money to repeat a vital shot.

Everyone around Billie was becoming aware of the effort she put into her role. She does worry on set, she does want to get it right and she is very aware of how many people in any given scene are depending on her. And they said that the pressure on *Doctor Who* was higher than on any of her previous jobs. 'There was a lot of pressure and filming with effects is very different to filming a soap or a sitcom where there are just a couple of people sitting in a room,' said *Doctor Who* extra Clive Kennet, who watched Billie tackle one of the most complex scenes in the show's seventh episode, 'The Long Game'. 'The process is simply more complicated and you need to have faith in everyone around you to pull it off. What the director tells you to do may seem ridiculous, in your logical mind, but it all comes together in the editing and the special-effects suite. As an actor on a show like *Doctor Who*, you have to accept that your job is going to seem very weird sometimes.'

For Billie, this weirdness brought its own sets of problems, not least because the more complicated the scene, the more nervous she got. 'I've been really terrible at stunts,' she admitted after the first few shows were in the bag. 'Every time I have done one, I have messed it up and ended up trashing the set and props. I've been so bruised and I've broken so many props, it's a joke. I just look at a prop and I start shaking – and so does the prop.'

Fortunately, as Billie's confidence grew, she fell even more in love with the wonderful world of sci-fi filming. 'It's knackering but it is a load of fun,' she said. 'It's kind of what you would wish for as a kid. It's also quite weird, getting up in the morning and thinking, "Here we go… off to save the world again." For me, though, the best thing is working as an actress every day. That's what I have wanted to do since I was a kid, so I'm still so thrilled to be living that particular dream.'

The effects in *Doctor Who* were extraordinary from the start. Everyone was aware that, in the Harry Potter age, the locations and villains had to be something special. So Billie, Christopher and all the others went from a new New York, through Victorian Cardiff, London in the Blitz and the edge of the universe. They fought against Autons disguised as mannequins, the reptilian Slitheens and, of course, Daleks (this time able not just to get up stairs but to fly).

Humour was also in plentiful supply — in the killer wheelie bins in Episode One as much as in the scripts. Overall, as the film extra Clive put it, 'It was hard work, but great fun. You felt like you were part of something really special every day and that's not a feeling you get on every set nowadays.'

But what would the public's reaction be when the series was finally aired? Tension had been building up for some time as the final day's filming and editing was carried out. The huge number of long-term *Doctor Who* fans — known as the Who-ies — were stoking up plenty of interest and the BBC's publicity machine was ready to move into top gear. Having spent so much time and money on the series, they were determined not to see it fail. The idea was to generate as many headlines as possible about the show in the weeks prior to its launch, and everyone knew that, after her split from Chris, no one made the headlines quite like Billie.

What worried the media office was whether their star was prepared to play ball – and whether it was ethical to ask her. As a singer, Billie had said that it was the marketing and promotion rather than the performing that had ground her down and forced her out of the industry at just 18. Four years on, there were worries that she would feel the same about promoting her acting career, so the press office trod carefully when they suggested some pre-publicity work. As it turned out, though, they needn't have been so worried. Billie was well aware of her obligations to the show and was more than happy to climb aboard this particular promotional treadmill. *Doctor Who* was something she was intensely proud to be part of. It had saved her sanity when she and Chris Evans split up and she didn't want anyone saying she hadn't done her bit to make it a success.

Fortunately, she had no problem charming the press. 'People like Billie. She is a decidedly sunny presence, often self-deprecating, bright, articulate and eager to please,' says *Times* reporter Garry Jenkins, who met her in a cool Soho hotel at the start of her new media offensive. But he noticed one big difference between this Billie Piper and the relentlessly well-groomed version who had met the press in her pop days. This time, she clearly wasn't forced to worry what she looked like. Just before heading down to meet Garry, she had spotted a cigarette burn hole in her sleeve. The old Billie (who always smoked, long before it was legal for her to do so) would have changed her clothes on the spot. The new one simply went down for the interview as she was. 'It is just not those kind of things that are important in life,' she says. 'That is one of things that Chris taught me and I won't ever forget it.'

That said, Billie was equally prepared to turn on the glamour when required. So she jumped at the chance to pick some of the sexiest Alexander McQueen and Azzedine Alaia clothes for a glossy photo-shoot in *Arena* magazine. The shoot itself went brilliantly – the hair and make-up staff in particular saying Billie was a pleasure to deal with. But, afterwards, Billie worried that some of the shots might have gone a bit too far – and seeing herself posing on the lad's mag cover lying on satin sheets in black underwear and being described as 'everyone's favourite jail bait emerging from a sex TARDIS' took the edge off the experience a little bit. Having some of the raciest shots reproduced in the tabloids alongside all the usual headlines of 'DOCTOR PHWOAR!', 'SEXTERMINATE!' and 'DALEK-TABLE' also gave the men on her dad's latest building site in Swindon something to talk about when their boss was away. They said they hadn't had so much to look at and joke about since the topless pictures of the boss's daughter on holiday in the Indian Ocean had been published the previous January.

The next downside for Billie came when all the usual

comics got on the case. 'How can anyone who once shared a bed with a man as ginger and ugly as Chris Evans ever really persuade us that she can be afraid of any other ugly monster ever again?' asked one. Then came some of the self-inflicted upsets Billie could perhaps have foreseen. She came in for a wave of criticism among die-hard fans when she did a question and answer session on XFM Radio and had to admit she didn't know who Davros was (he's the radiation-damaged scientist who created the Daleks). So, for future interviews, she made sure she knew exactly what TARDIS stood for (Time And Relative Dimension In Space, if you're asking) and prepared to face the critics head on. 'I didn't grow up with *Doctor Who*, but it is not just about pleasing the old fans, it is about bringing a new group to the table. I don't think we have to be too hung up on that. The show keeps the essence of *Doctor Who*, but it is a different time. People have changed.'

In March, the publicity campaign for the show reached its climax with the official press launch for the series. And absolutely no expense, or imagination, had been spared. A professional events company had built a mock-up of the TARDIS in the lobby of the five-star St David's Hotel on Cardiff Bay (which had pretty much been Billie's full-time home for the past few months). After walking through the TARDIS, reporters were served canapés, watched over by a couple of circling Daleks as the subtly modernised theme tune echoed around them. Then there was a mini-screening, and then the main event — a roving press conference for the stars. Some 300 reporters were there, and Billie ended up being asked more questions than anyone else on the small circular tables dotted around the room for interviews — much to the relief of the famously media-shy Christopher Eccleston.

Putting on such a show for the press had been a huge effort for Billie, though. Just days earlier, when the treadmill of filming *Doctor Who* had finally slowed down, *Independent* writer Craig McLean said he was shocked at how exhausted and drained its female lead appeared to be. 'She was smiley and friendly, but looked washed out. Pale and largely make-up free, her eyes were that of a junkie panda and her complexion was spotty. Her hair was stringy, her roots badly needing a touch-up.' She scrubbed up well, though and, at the press launch, Craig says he hardly recognised her new glossy incarnation. He also told any of his readers who might have missed her acting renaissance of the previous year that they would be in for a surprise with her performance in *Doctor Who*. 'She's smiling, she's sane, she's sober. Meet Billie Piper: Serious Actor. Who knew?' he wrote as the big day approached.

Saturday, 26 March 2005 was the day everyone found out whether all the time, effort and money had been worthwhile and, as evening approached, Billie had no idea how to spend the night. She felt too stir-crazy to stay in at home and watch it and said she was torn between going to a pub to watch it among a crowd of strangers and going to a TV-free pub to pretend it was just another Saturday night. In the event, she picked the latter option and sank more than a few drinks to try and take her mind off the show. She then remembered her showbusiness responsibilities and headed to The Ivy for a late dinner with her family. But she was very aware of how big the revived show had suddenly become. She and Christopher were on the cover of the *Radio Times* and on almost every other television magazine and newspaper supplement going. 'It is hard to get your head around the size of *Doctor Who* or the impression it has made. It scared the hell out of me, if I'm honest. I just wanted to get the first one out so it could settle down and just be part of Saturday night viewing.'

As it turned out, the quality of the writing, acting and production meant the show remained a cut above the rest and never quite turned into mainstream Saturday night television – amazingly enough, it was considered enough of a news story for Billie to be invited to face Jeremy Paxman on *Newsnight* to talk about its success. And as the weeks went by, the critics piled ever more praise on almost everyone involved. One key word which seemed to sum a lot of it up was witty. The humour was often far more intelligent than you might expect and everyone's timing in delivering the gags seemed spot on. Former Doctor Who Sylvester McCoy, who had been in the lead role in 1987 with Sophie Aldred playing his teenage assistant Ace, was hugely enthusiastic about the show and how it had evolved. 'Just as *Doctor Who* in the 1960s reflected the way in which Britain was swinging, exploding out of a cocoon of post-war gloominess, this shows the exciting, extraordinary London of 2005. I loved it,' he said after lavishing particular praise on Billie.

Other long-established fans of the series were given plenty to look forward to as well – including some sly winks to past episodes that most first-time viewers would miss. Take the early scene where an Internet search threw up images of Eccleston's Doctor standing on the infamous grassy knoll in Dallas, Texas. This was specifically filmed as an unspoken reference to the fact that the very first episode of the show, back in 1963, had been broadcast on the day President Kennedy was shot in Dallas. It had to be repeated the following week because so many people had either missed it or been distracted from it as the news from America broke.

For Billie, being part of such a multi-layered, superbly produced and critically acclaimed show should have made 2004 and 2005 the very best years of her life – but the end of her marriage meant that, for all the success in her career, she could never see those years in that light. 'Life is never as straightforward as you think it is going to be,' the former Doctor's assistant Anneke Willis had warned her. And after losing Chris, Billie was to get another reminder of just how true those words had become. She was about to say goodbye to one of her newest and closest of friends.

13
A NEW DOCTOR

AT FIRST GLANCE, Billie and Christopher Eccleston made unlikely soulmates. She was seen as the lightweight former pop star whose past history suggested she was happy to live her life in the limelight. He was always described as the older, gruffer and intensely private man who wanted to push himself as an actor and suffer silently for his art. When they first met, in the audition room and again on the *Doctor Who* set, they admit that they brought those perceptions and prejudices to the table. But they soon threw them aside. What brought the pair together was the fact that both Billie and Christopher are very different to their public personas. And it turned out that the real people beneath the masks found they stood on a huge amount of common ground.

'Christopher and I shared a lot during the past eight months,' Billie said after the first series was in the bag.

'We had heavy schedules and personal lives and we have been joined at the hip. We have a very intense kind of relationship. We get on famously. It was instant — it just worked straight away.'

Christopher, meanwhile, spoke just as highly of his young co-star and predicted that they will remain friends for ever. But after just one episode of the new series had been broadcast in March 2005, it was announced that Christopher wanted out of the show. Billie would be acting alongside a different Doctor in the second series, which had almost simultaneously been given the green light by the BBC.

The news was a huge shock for fans who had finally warmed to Christopher's often stark interpretation of the revived Doctor. It also triggered a wave of confusion inside the BBC. At first, the corporation put out a statement saying that Christopher feared being typecast and had found the series gruelling to film — a statement it was then forced to retract as unauthorised and untrue. But whatever Christopher's real reasons for the departure might have been, Russell T Davies admitted that everyone on the crew was 'tense and jittery' about the future — especially when rumours suddenly hit the press saying Billie might jump TARDIS alongside her Doctor.

She happily went on record to deny the reports and said she was looking forward to coming back as Rose in the second series. But who would she be acting alongside? Bill Nighy, Eddie Izzard and Alan Davies were all said to be in the frame. But *Casanova* and *Blackpool* star David Tennant was widely seen as the front runner and, on 16 April 2005, that news was confirmed. It gave Billie some much needed security about the future in a year that was still being shaped by the turmoil of her split from Chris.

What worried many people was the fact that when she was away from the *Doctor Who* set, Billie still didn't seem to have as many friends as you might imagine. Her whole life seemed marked by leaving people with whom she might otherwise have bonded. She left her Swindon secondary school just after joining it to head to London and Sylvia Young's. She left that school nearly two years ahead of her original schedule to join the very grown-up world of pop music, and she left the music business to live in her former husband's shadow alongside his mostly middle-aged, almost exclusively male friends. Three of these golfing and drinking pals had even come along on her first major holiday with Chris in Madeira at the end of 2000. The thirty- and forty-something men were rarely far away from then on. 'The wedding video footage was famously chilling, with the tiny bride being shepherded down the aisle by Evans and another middle-aged DJ, Danny Baker,' wrote *Times* reporter Lucy Alexander after seeing the images of Billie's big day in Vegas. Divorce counsellors say that working out who gets custody of joint friends is very far from a joke – but, as far as Billie was concerned, the middle-aged faces who had drifted in and out of her marriage could stay with her former husband. The problem was that this left precious few friendly faces for her.

Even when her marriage was at its most blissful, Billie had frequently been spotted buying single tickets for the cinema — although she claimed it was because she could relax more by not needing to worry about her companion's reactions to the film, rather than because she couldn't find a friend to go with. That said, she was perhaps photographed in supermarkets buying meals-for-one a little too often in her post-Chris days to fully reassure those concerned about her welfare. The other worry for her fans was the fact that she seemed to struggle to let go of the man who had turned her life around back in 2000.

Shortly after their split was made official, Chris proved that he had come up with a unique way to cast off some painful memories of his marriage. He famously rented a stall at Camden market in north London and put a huge number of his possessions up for sale.

'I'm clearing all my stuff from all my homes and making a fresh start. All my stuff around here has painful memories. I'm just doing this to get rid of the headache,' he said. The stall obviously turned into a big news story and Chris was happy to guide reporters through its ever-changing contents. 'It is about clearing the table and starting afresh. All these things were bought when we were together and did have sentimental value. Of course, the furniture here has memories. Everywhere I look, I see Billie. There's a black leather sofa that used to belong

to Bob Dylan where we sat and cuddled and watched
TV. There are the treadmills that Billie used to work out
on. All that kind of thing has to go.'

To her credit, Billie was immediately ready to support
her former husband. On a rare day off from the *Doctor
Who* set, she turned up on his first day as a market
trader, chatting and helping for 20 minutes and then
giving him a hug and a kiss when she thought the
photographers weren't looking. She also wrote, 'Be a
happy chappy… XX' on the whitewashed wall behind
the stall as a memento.

Moving on and letting go was proving difficult, not
least because Billie had been out of the dating game for
some time. 'I always see the good in people and I'm
quite naïve. People say blokes try to chat me up
sometimes, but I never know when they are doing it.
I'm a very tactile person and, if guys are like that back,
I just think they are being friendly. Anyway, you forget
what it is like to go on dates and converse with men in
a different way again. It's all a bit strange,' she admitted.
And in the lull after their split, Billie liked the idea of
some good old-fashioned dating. She happily admits she
is a born romantic, watching *Love Actually* twice as her
own love life fell apart. 'I was crying… howling… I
completely lost control. And I don't cry easily,' she said
afterwards, claiming she was once again pleased to have
been in the cinema on her own.

What made matters worse was a sudden and hugely
cruel burst of Billie-baiting which had suddenly sprung

up in some of the big celebrity magazines. Her complexion has never been perfect and she happily admits it gets worse when she is working hard, under pressure or miserable. With all three scenarios hitting her at once in late 2004 and early 2005, it was little wonder that she didn't always look her best. But it was surely no excuse for the intrusive photographs which zoomed in on her face and made her wonder if she would ever be in the papers again without some tasteless 'spot of bother' style pun in the picture caption.

One person she discovered she could rely on in her post-Chris days was the famously single *Little Britain* star David Walliams. She shared a series of dinners with him and joined him at a Kylie Minogue concert in Earl's Court, west London. But for all the celebrity columnists' talk of romance, the truth was that their relationship was mainly about business. Billie was a long-term fan of David's show; he was a long-term fan of her acting. So could he and his comedy partner Matt Lucas find a cameo role for her?

A role as Vicky Pollard's super-chav arch enemy was being fleshed out as she and David enjoyed each other's company in 2005. The 2006 Christmas Special and the final series the duo were hoping to write in 2007 would tell if it might ever see the light of day.

Apart from David, Billie was also linked, equally falsely, to *Doctor Who* co-star Noel Clarke and *Coupling* actor Alastair Southey. There were even fantastically over-the-top reports that she had found a new bloke with the tabloid-friendly name of Basher (he turned out to be the ex-boyfriend of a friend and was never more than an occasional clubbing partner for Billie). Then, of course, there were all the usual rumours that she and Chris were actually back together. 'We are reconciled and spent the night together... it was great,' Billie allegedly told 'a friend' according to one newspaper back in November 2004. But they weren't, they hadn't and the 'friend' didn't exist.

It was exactly the same when similar claims about a reconciliation were raised around six months later. A girl Chris started seeing after his split fanned the flames by saying Billie was constantly in her former partner's mind. 'It was obvious he still had feelings. When he wasn't chatting to her on the phone, he was taking about her to me,' she said. And, after a while, Billie was forced to address the deep, ongoing connection between her and Chris. She did so by accepting just how odd it must look to outsiders, but saying it was entirely right for them.

'I always thought it was weird when exes hung out together. Now I am doing it myself, I understand it,' she said. 'We've been through such a lot. There's been no pressure. It is almost nicer now because there are no harboured feelings, no resentment. We are best of buds and always will be,' she added, confirming the thoughts she had voiced when they first separated.

What Billie was also able to confirm was that another face from her past was now very much part of her present. As she threw herself back into the single life during the final month's filming on *Doctor Who*, she met up with a group of people from her days at Innocent Records. Several were still in the music industry and had plenty of good gossip and stories to help take their former colleague's mind of her troubles. But one of them was now living a completely different life — and Billie found she had an instant connection with him.

His name was Amadu Sowe. Five years older than Billie, he had been born in north London to a Spanish mother and an Egyptian father. It was exactly the kind of exotic parentage that the adventure-seeking Billie had dreamed of having when she was desperate to shake off the conventionality of her own Swindon childhood. She had first met Amadu more than seven years earlier at Innocent. Back then, Billie had thought she wanted to be the world's most famous pop star; Amadu had thought he wanted to be a major behind-the-scenes player in the music world. He was working as a publicist for their parent company, Virgin, and was convinced that he had what it took to get to the top of that most precarious of industries.

But something had changed for him, just as something had changed for Billie. Around the same time as she became disillusioned with the business of performing as a pop star, so Amadu got disillusioned with the business of promoting them. And less than a year after Billie escaped from the business with Chris Evans, her handsome former colleague escaped to study Law at Reading University. Meeting up again seven years later in his final year at law school gave them both the opportunity to re-examine why they had made the choices that they had. Their other friends were pretty much ignored as they relived all the reasons why they had wanted out of the music business. Billie was hugely impressed by the way Amadu had followed his dreams, defied the odds and turned his life around. Amadu felt exactly the same about her. But would he have the guts to ask her out?

For a while, he held back, fearing he might be reading things wrong or that Billie might be too much on the rebound from Chris. But after a bit of nudging from friends, he took a chance – and Billie agreed straight away.

Over the coming months, Billie and Amadu were going to spend more and more time together. It would be Billie's first slow-burn relationship – but it seemed all the stronger for that. They went to yoga classes on some of their earliest dates, and on many occasions Billie was happy just to sit with Amadu in a café or, as the weather improved, on the grass of Primrose Hill as he focused on his law books and prepared for his final exams.

For all this, the relationship wasn't always as conventional as it appeared. Princess Diana famously said there were three people in her marriage to Prince Charles; Amadu was to find that there seemed to be an equal number in his love affair with Billie – and the third person, of course, was Chris Evans.

Less than six months after the news of their split had broken, Billie and Chris still seemed to be living in each other's pockets. And much of the ongoing Billie and Chris show was being played out in front of the cameras. When Chris made his big entertainment comeback in February 2005 by hosting the 25th Brit Awards, for example, Billie sat at his table between his mother and Paul Gascoigne. 'It is a really special night for me and Billie would have killed me if I hadn't asked her to be part of it,' Chris said afterwards.

When leaving Earl's Court after the show, they were both heading in the same direction – because after moving out of the huge Belsize Park house she had shared with him, Billie moved less than 100 yards down the road. She then returned to her former marital home almost daily, because her new flat didn't have a parking space, so Chris let her leave her car in their old driveway. She had just bought a white 1989 Porsche 911 with black leather seats and white piping – 'I've got an obsession with boy-racer cars which dates back to hanging around in Swindon,' she said.

Chris, rather than Amadu, was also the first person Billie asked for advice when a house opposite came on the market and she needed to work out if it was worth buying. The pair wandered across the road together and spent nearly an hour examining the house with an estate agent. It was only when Billie finally moved that Amadu got to help out, and even then Chris was, quite literally, in the picture alongside him. One of the items the paparazzi snapped him carrying out of the removal van and into his girlfriend's new house was a huge framed photograph of Chris, wearing a sunhat and his trademark glasses.

Slightly less personal were the next set of pictures Amadu carried into her new house – a couple of equally large framed Sex Pistols posters. The one big item that wasn't on view that day was a Dalek. Billie had joked that she had to restrain herself almost every day from taking a sonic screwdriver home from the *Doctor Who* set and said she thought a Dalek would make a fantastic talking point in her new hall. Sadly, the producers were not yet ready to let one go so, until they relented, her souvenir hunt had to be limited to some bracelets one of the set designers made out of the wires that sprung out of the TARDIS.

Giving the gossip columnists even more to talk about the day of her house move, Billie was frequently spotted going back into her former marital home to get some glasses of water and cups of tea for the removal men. Her utterly relaxed relationship with Chris was still raising eyebrows – and when he appeared on *Parkinson* shortly after the move, Chris accepted that everyone, probably including Amadu, could be forgiven for being confused by it. 'Living so close to each other is a strange situation. I don't expect other people to understand it because I don't understand it either. But we get on extraordinarily well and we love each other… so there it is.'

Fortunately for Billie, she had privately explained all this to Amadu, and he had told her it would never be a problem. 'He is very good because Chris and I are pretty much inseparable. I told him when we first started going out that Chris and I had this very special thing and I was never going to give it up, so he would have to accept it.' So when he was studying, Amadu had no problem seeing his girlfriend head out for an evening with her ex-husband – and didn't even care when he then read in the tabloids about how they had been spotted sitting on the edge of Hampstead Heath eating fish and chips as if they were still a dream couple.

To his enormous credit, Amadu had total faith in his girlfriend's affections and, having deliberately walked away from the celebrity world and the promotional mind games when he had been at Virgin, he had no wish to rejoin it now. He wanted to be with his girlfriend, but he wanted to remain in the background.

They were sentiments that Billie herself was increasingly coming to understand. 'I have learned a lot about fame, chiefly that I have become completely indifferent to it,' she said amidst all the *Doctor Who*-inspired madness. 'I love my job as an actress and I fully understand its requirements, but I am not interested in having a public life.' Neither did she want to foist one on an equally unwilling Amadu. 'With Chris, things did obviously get a bit crazy with all the press attention and I am not particularly keen on crazy. Now I don't want to talk about Amadu too much because I don't want my life encroaching on his any more than it has to.'

Quiet dinners out, occasional trips to the cinema, lunches with friends, long evenings at home. That was the very private way the couple wanted to live – though even this was put in jeopardy when one extraordinary rumour broke. An unnamed friend apparently said Amadu was 'a Tantric sex expert who can go for hours and hours'. From then on, the tabloids were in seventh heaven. It didn't seem to matter that no one could really remember where or how the rumour had begun; it stuck, and was repeated almost every time the papers mentioned Amadu's name – even Michael Parkinson talked about it when Chris Evans came on his show.

And Amadu? Yes, it was all a little bit embarrassing for someone who wanted to keep a low profile. But as he was the first to admit, there are worse rumours than this one. And joking about his supposed prowess in the bedroom made for a lot of funny conversations everywhere else.

What might surprise people who only read the celebrity magazines and just saw pictures of Billie driving her car, in pub gardens or supermarkets was that she was also still working. Her next professional role was in a series which echoed the updated *Canterbury Tales* revival, which had first earned her good reviews as an actress. The BBC had decided to get some of the same top writers to add an equally modern twist to a selection of Shakespeare's classic plays. Peter Bowker, for example, who had cast Billie and been blown away by her performance in his adaptation of *The Miller's Tale*, was re-writing *A Midsummer Night's Dream*, which sadly didn't have an obvious role for the actress. But one of the other authors in the team, *Cold Feet* writer David Nicholls, felt he had something she might be interested in. He was taking a fresh look at *Much Ado About Nothing* and wanted to move the original setting from renaissance Sicily to a modern-day local television station. The role of Hero, the bright, innocent love interest, was transformed into an Ulrika-style weather girl; it seemed perfect for Billie and, after a couple of meetings and informal read-throughs with the producers, she signed up for the job. 'The script was a corker, every line was so funny and, when I heard who else was involved, I knew it was going to be a great project,' she said.

What Billie also liked was the framework into which David was putting his reinvented plot. He said he wanted it to have a sense of the golden age of Hollywood about it, to hint at the big Cary Grant and Katherine Hepburn films such as *The Philadelphia Story* and *Bringing Up Baby*, as well as the more contemporary comedies like *Four Weddings and a Funeral* and *When Harry Met Sally*. As a huge fan of classic films and all romantic comedies, Billie was pretty much sold on the project from this moment on.

Filming *Much Ado* was a short, intense and surprisingly complicated affair. The producers hadn't been given the biggest budget in the world so the entire, multi-location show had to be filmed in just 21 days. There was no room for any mistakes, but there was plenty of scope for everyone to pitch in with ideas to help them get the look and feel right as quickly – and cheaply – as possible.

Afterwards, everybody said this enforced teamwork

helped bring everyone together and turn the show into a surprisingly enjoyable experience. 'It was a really happy shoot and I hope that shows on the film,' said the BBC's Drama Series and Serials Producer Diederick Santer. 'If the audience experience even a tiny fraction of the fun we had making the programme then I am sure they will enjoy themselves tremendously.'

Billie was on a high from the start, not least because anything that didn't involve running away from sci-fi monsters felt like a walk in the park after *Doctor Who*. The trickiest part of her role, and a big part of the fun of the story, were her character's struggles to pronounce some of the complex meteorological terms – not least the word 'meteorology' itself. Again, Billie was more prepared than the writers had expected, though. 'After *Doctor Who*, I was getting used to saying words I had never used in my life before so I was getting better at pronouncing all the difficult ones,' she said. 'And on *Doctor Who*, a lot of Russell's bizarre words are made up, so if you can handle them you can handle anything.'

There was a big ensemble cast in the show, working alongside Billie and the adaptation's two main stars, *Cutting It* actress Sarah Parish and *Band of Brothers* star Damian Lewis, as the bickering lovers Beatrice and Benedick. Just before filming began, Sarah spent two days in the BBC's *South Today* newsroom to get a feel for her role, while Billie met up with one of the *BBC Breakfast* weather girls for some inside advice. 'She taught me how you hold yourself and present yourself on screen and I also got to grips with the speaking rhythm that news reporters use, the kind of intonation they have. Then I just sat at home watching daytime television for a week telling everyone I was doing research.'

On set, Billie says her two personal highlights both involved dressing up. First, she got to wear the kind of big white wedding dress she had never worn in real life. Then she was given an even better chance to put on a show. Hero was given a full Marilyn Monroe-style costume – exactly the same kind of dress and wig combination Billie herself had once worn at a fancy-dress party. 'I love that scene from *The Seven Year Itch* with the white dress and Marilyn has always been one of my heroes. I felt right at home in that costume.'

The penultimate day of filming was the first time the cast and crew headed out on the road for some location work. Their first stop was West Wittering near Chichester and then they moved down to Brighton for a day's filming on the seafront (which was doubling up as Bournemouth). The wrap party was also held in Brighton and, after such a short, high-pressure shoot, it was a wonderful chance for everyone to relax. 'We all gelled and every single minute of every single day was brilliant. It was such a laugh – funwise, it was the best job I have had,' Sarah Parish said afterwards.

So did *Much Ado About Nothing* work as a modern re-telling of a 450-year-old play? When shooting finished, everyone on the set hoped they had created something good, though it would be several months before their work was fully edited and ready for transmission. In the meantime, Billie was hoping for the best. She admits that, like many children, she was almost totally disinterested in Shakespeare before arriving at stage school and having her eyes opened to how strong the plots and the language were. 'I hope that by retelling it in a modern way, a new audience will get interested in Shakespeare as well,' she said.

But long before she was to find out if her message would get across, she had another huge challenge on her hands. The summer was heating up and it was almost time to head back to Wales. The second series of *Doctor Who* was ready to be filmed.

14
BACK IN BUSINESS

GOING BACK TO Cardiff in the summer of 2005 obviously brought back some upsetting memories for Billie. A year earlier she had been a completely different woman, with little idea that her marriage was about to hit the rocks. Now, she felt secure and happy in her new relationship with Amadu. But could she really rely on it going the distance?

Deep down, she could hardly fail to worry that history might repeat itself as her workload cranked up to breaking point once more. She was due to be working on a Christmas Special and another 13 episodes of the show over another eight-month period. The gruelling 12-hour days and 11-day fortnights were set to begin all over again. Life would once more be centred around Cardiff rather than her London home with Amadu.

Fortunately, he was determined to give his girlfriend

all the support she needed. Amadu headed over to Cardiff with her on her first week back at work and they both joined writer and actor Stephen Fry and the rest of the *Doctor Who* production team at a Cardiff restaurant for a welcome dinner in honour of David Tennant. It was a relaxed and happy night and, just before midnight, a beaming Billie left hand-in-hand with Amadu, convinced that David would make a great Doctor and a good friend.

He turned out to be thinking exactly the same. 'I didn't know Billie before I joined the cast, but I had been admiring her in the show,' David told reporters after his first day. 'She is just great, fantastic, absolutely perfect for the part. Spunky and quick and sexy, just the ideal companion, really. So I am very pleased that she is going to do the whole series,' he added, putting paid to yet another set of rumours that Rose was to be written out after a couple of episodes at Billie's request.

What David also said was that he immediately felt the same pressure that Billie had experienced the previous year. 'The worst bit of being the new guy on set was all the hoo-haa that comes with the show – the fact that everybody is so fascinated by it. That makes it the most wonderful job in the world, but also the most terrifying. When I finished my first day of filming, I remember going home and collapsing. Everything had been building up and it was exhausting.'

One of the team's first tasks was to film the fantastic 2006 Christmas Special. Most of it was put together over the course of ten uncharacteristically hot July days in Cardiff and on an industrial park in west London – the snow falling on and around the TARDIS obviously being false. And to use the most obvious pun in the television reviewers' handbook, the episode was a cracker. The killer Christmas trees and scary Santas threatened to steal the show, although most of the focus was, of course, on the performance and style of the new Doctor. Everyone wanted to know exactly what he would be like, and that, of course, included Billie's Rose. 'Can I just say, travelling with you – I just love it! You're so different,' was one of her first lines with the new man in charge.

In real life, the pair were obviously getting on well. They had already given several joint press conferences to promote the new show and the journalists said they were clearly relaxed and happy in each other's company. In a matter of months, they knew each other inside out and had plenty of in-jokes to share. 'My nickname for David Tennant is David Ten-inch. But I have no grounds for calling him that. I just find it funny,' she told reporters with a trademark, wide smile. David, of course, was thrilled.

After meeting Amadu on his first day at work, he had also met most of Billie's family and she said he was on course to be 'a friend for life'. Both pointed out that they saw more of each other than they did of anyone else, including many of the other cast members. 'We are the two constants in the show, so we are in rehearsal, on set and in camera together pretty much every day. It's nice to spend time with the other regular characters when they have scenes but sometimes we don't see those guys for ages,' said David.

'That's why I see David more, much more, than I see my family or my boyfriend,' Billie added.

The first episode of the second series, due to be shown more than three months after the Christmas Special, was called 'New Earth'. It was set early in the 5,000,000th century and saw the Doctor and Rose arrive at the new home of the human race following the destruction of planet Earth. Zoe Wanamaker was back as villainess-in-chief Lady Cassandra, Russell T Davies was in the writer's chair and it was a superb start to the series. But everyone knew that much of the audience's focus would still be on the new Doctor and the way he interacted with his assistant. What soon became clear was that it wasn't just a different leading man at the TARDIS controls. Billie's character seemed subtly different as well. Fans said the new Rose came over as more confident, less terrified of the monsters and situations she encounters, and far more at ease in the new Doctor's company.

The vital dynamic between the two leads was working well from the start. David's clever deadpan delivery was one factor in the new deal. 'Many things about this are not good,' he would say, eyebrows raised, in the face of some new monster-laden horror. The production and editing staff on set loved it. When they examined the early scenes and got ready to turn them into a broadcast-quality show, they were convinced that they were on to a winner. They were looking at perfect chemistry, a perfectly pitched relationship and a new Doctor who was a perfect match for Billie.

After the huge success of the first series, it was little wonder that the producers had managed to line up some fantastic guest stars for the second. So Billie's next set of scripts had her acting alongside many of her professional heroes, from Zoe Wanamaker in the very first episode of the new series to Maureen Lipman, Pauline Collins, Peter Kay and *Buffy* to *Little Britain* star Anthony Head. As ever, there was also plenty of humour – often at Billie's expense. The writers tapped into the public perception of their star and she was happy to have everyone laugh along with it.

'Oh, my God – I'm a Chav!' Zoe Wanamaker said as Lady Cassandra, after her spirit had been transferred into Rose's body halfway through the show. 'It's like living inside a bouncy castle,' she added after getting a feel for her new, much fuller figure.

Even more fun came when Peter Kay joined the cast in the *Love and Monsters* episode. 'I actually had to inflict pain on myself with pinches to stop myself from laughing. He is brilliant but he destroyed a lot of scenes by being just too funny for me,' Billie said.

Other episodes in the second series would ultimately make waves and headlines for different reasons. 'Our writer, Russell T Davies, has moved the scripts on – they are really terrifying,' Billie said of many of them. 'Some deal with the Devil in a very spooky way. They are very dark, in a good way, and very, very thought-provoking.'

The key to the show was the clever mix of light amidst that darkness, though. And one way the team produced this was to keep the 'are they, aren't they?' questions about the Doctor and his assistant's relationship bubbling away at all times. Somehow, it was far easier to see Billie and David together than it had been to see her and Christopher. And there was a groundswell of opinion that viewers might be ready for the first full-blown, in-TARDIS love story. Rumours of an on-screen kiss started to build up. 'Screen kisses? I love them, especially with David,' Billie said, giving away the plot by saying that it had taken three takes to perfect her first big kiss with her co-star (and giving what most people might have felt was too much information by admitting, 'We didn't do tongues, because that day we had been eating egg and cress sandwiches for lunch.')

As it would turn out, the Doctor–Rose romance was to go off the boil pretty soon after their big kiss, giving Billie a real chance to prove her worth as an actress. There was a huge poignancy in two subsequent episodes. The first was 'School Reunion' where the Doctor first reacquainted himself with a lonely yet dignified former assistant Sarah Jane Smith, played by Elizabeth Sladen. Sarah Jane had clearly loved the Doctor from the moment she had met him – and had waited for him from the moment that he had left her.

Seeing Billie's Rose deal with an unexpected rival

made for a surprisingly moving episode, and Billie's emotions took full reign again just one week later in 'The Girl in the Fireplace', when the Doctor really did fall in love, with Madame de Pompadour, played by actress Sophia Myles.

As Rose, Billie's response to both these events was a minor revelation. It was genuinely possible to see the emotions play out on her face – the confusion and the sudden realisation of what is going on, the shock at the strength of her own feelings, the embarrassment and the pain of her rejection. Writer Russell T Davies's promise that the show would be a drama, rather than light entertainment, had never been better demonstrated.

Behind the scenes, something else was going on. Love was in the air in Wales as summer turned to autumn and several romances were blossoming in the rare waking hours that everyone spent away from the set. David Tennant was falling for his Madame de Pompadour co-star Sophia Myles, and Billie was finding out that Amadu was a man who could keep his promises. He and his law books headed over to Cardiff almost every weekend throughout the shoot, and he sometimes headed over for occasional evenings when there was a work function Billie was nervous about attending on her own. He also had no problem dealing with his girlfriend's temporary unsociability. On her rare full weekends off, Billie said she was hardly a bundle of fun as a companion. 'I just sit on the sofa for two days. I don't really want to talk to anyone at the weekends. I like to sit in my flat and be completely selfish. I watch TV, eat far too much and drink some beers.'

With his final exams approaching, this actually worked pretty well for the pair of them. Amadu could sit with his notes in the next room revising – making for some surprisingly pleasant and supportive weekends. It was certainly a far cry from the Billie of old and a huge sign of how much her life had changed. Reporter Rachel Cooke from the *Observer* was one of the first outsiders to spot this new maturity. She says Billie finally seemed to have a genuine sense of inner confidence and calm, two things she had always been forced to fake in her pop days. 'When you meet Billie now, you realise that the person trapped inside her peachy body is actually a middle-aged woman,' Rachel concluded – and she was at pains to say she meant this as a very big compliment.

Amadu's studying paid off in the autumn when he got the news that he had passed his law degree and, after a night out to celebrate, he and Billie booked a week away in the New Year when their workloads would finally allow them to relax properly. Before then, Billie had plenty to do – and a lot of it was making her nervous.

The first big test came on Tuesday, 25 October 2005. It was the night of the *National Television Awards* and Billie had been nominated as Most Popular Actress alongside Caroline Quentin and *EastEnders'* stars Jessie Wallace and June Brown. Having won so many major awards as a pop star, many people might have thought Billie would have taken this next awards ceremony in her stride. But she couldn't. Being recognised as an actress mattered hugely to her. This was what, where and who she had always wanted to be. So as she wandered around at home all day trying to decide what to wear, she reckoned she was probably the most nervous woman in London.

After endlessly looking through her wardrobe, Billie decided some good old-fashioned glamour could help her get through the night. She wore a short, black, figure-hugging dress for the ceremony – and it paid off. She won the award, looked a million dollars as she headed for the stage to collect it and immediately proved that the old Billie was still very much in evidence by almost spitting her chewing gum out of her perfectly made-up mouth during her acceptance speech.

'Thank you so much… this means so much to me, I can't even begin to tell you,' she said, approaching tears after politicians David Davis and David Cameron had handed her the award.

Back at her table, Billie's colleagues had plenty to celebrate as well. The nominations had been for the first series of the show, so Christopher Eccleston was there and was named Most Popular Actor while *Doctor Who* itself was Most Popular Drama. 'I was shaking like a leaf and had to have a word with myself on the way to the stage because I thought I was going to cry properly, which would have been too embarrassing. It was a brilliant night, but I spent the whole evening in shock, chewing my nails,' Billie told the press afterwards.

As it turned out, the award could not have come at a better time. *Much Ado About Nothing* was finally going to be broadcast on BBC One and it would confirm that the judging panel at the *National Television Awards* had been spot on in naming Billie as Best Actress. *Much Ado About Nothing* and the whole *Shakespeare Re-Told* season was to get some great reviews, and Billie in particular was to get some superb ones.

The *Daily Telegraph* was one of the most effusive of the papers. Its main review read, 'Billie Piper's gorgeousness almost leaps off the screen. But, crucially, her beauty comes underpinned by genuine, no-nonsense niceness. And, like the rest of this sparking, often hilarious re-imagining of Shakespeare, she shows an artful knack for comedy, too.'

Almost every other critic agreed and the show was another hit addition to Billie's acting CV. But for all these very public plaudits, one far lower-profile review of *Much Ado* ended up meaning even more to Billie, however. It had been emailed to the BBC by a young girl and it proved the show had done exactly what Billie had hoped it might – it had generated a new respect for Shakespeare. 'It was great,' the young reviewer wrote. 'I have never read Shakespeare before but I watched it because I like Billie Piper. I am only 12 but I loved it.' It was exactly what Billie wanted to hear.

One other big show was being launched amidst a barrage of publicity in November 2005 but, despite Billie's best efforts, it was to prove far less successful.

Chris Evans was due back on screen. His new show, *OFI Sunday* (a cleverly titled echo to his breakthrough hit *TFI Friday*) had been commissioned by ITV. Billie was to be the star guest on his first show (with Amadu happy to sit in the audience and support her). She was also ready to be the butt of as many jokes as Chris could throw at her – and shrieked when he brought out the new Rose doll that was being sold on the back of the *Doctor Who* brand. 'I look like Master Splinter – the giant rat from Teenage Mutant Ninja Turtles! I know I've got big teeth but this really takes the mick. And I've got a gammy eye!' she screamed as she examined the doll in a moment of pure television gold.

But however much Billie threw herself into the jokes, the critics were in no mood to be kind. After praising his return to form as the host of the Brits, a new Chris Evans backlash was suddenly in full swing. 'Episode One had 3.7 million viewers and 3 million of them were probably only watching to see Billie Piper,' said the *Daily Mirror*. Other commentators were even harsher on the host. 'Watching *OFI Sunday* is akin to observing 100 years of popular light entertainment sink sobbing to its knees,' wrote online television critic Ian Jones. '*OFI Sunday's* first, but not its greatest, misdemeanour is to presume nothing has changed in television over the past decade. The mood, the pace, the volume, the structure – everything about the show reeks of the mid-1990s.'

The implication, everywhere, was that while Billie had moved on in her life and in her career, her former husband was stuck in a rut. *OFI Sunday* never made it into a second series, although Chris would soon prove his critics wrong by becoming a huge if unlikely hit with Radio Two listeners. Within six months of his television drubbing, he was named as the new host of the station's flagship 'drive-time' show, replacing the legendary Johnnie Walker. Chris was also in the money – in April 2006, news leaked out that he was earning £540,000 a year for the two-hour, Monday to Friday shows.

Back in Cardiff after her *OFI Sunday* appearance, Billie had her nose back on the *Doctor Who* grindstone. Despite claims in some papers, she certainly wasn't out partying and singing karaoke every night with local bad girl Charlotte Church, even though she had briefly rented an apartment in the same waterside block as the singer.

Cardiff and the local population, though, were becoming very close to Billie's heart. The number of fans of all ages who turned up hoping for photographs and autographs when the crew was out filming on location seemed to have grown rather than diminished in the 18 months that the stars had been there. And Billie and David were both enjoying constant praise in the local papers for their willingness to try and see as many fans as possible before and after the cameras started to roll.

What everyone liked about the arrangement was the very discreet and sensitive security that surrounded the show. The producers had made it clear that they wanted to deter the professional paparazzi who could distract the stars and spoil things for fans by leaking crucial plot lines.

But no one wanted to alienate the locals who were often putting up with street closures or other inconveniences as the Welsh streets were transformed into anything from Victorian warehouses to futuristic battlegrounds. It was a careful balancing act and it was managed successfully. 'People have been fantastic. We were sent some lovely little Dalek cakes from one of the people on the street where we filmed the other one day which was really touching,' Billie said. She and David were often spotted in the bars and bistros of the redeveloped dockside and were called on to turn on the city's Christmas lights as the Series Two filming schedule drew to a close.

Christmas itself brought a real joy for Billie. 'As a child, Christmas was all about waiting for the day's big television show to come on – normally *Only Fools and Horses*. I was over the moon when I found out that our Christmas Special was going to be broadcast on the day itself rather than just in Christmas week. It made me feel incredibly proud,' she said.

There was more to be proud of just around the corner. In January, the *Harry Potter* star Daniel Radcliffe handed Billie the Breakthrough Award at the high-brow *South Bank Show Awards* in London. This time, Billie really did find it impossible to stop the tears as she approached the podium. No one could forget how much she had gone through in the past few years, or how much she had achieved amidst such turmoil. It was something she could hardly fail to acknowledge in her acceptance speech. 'This has been the most emotional year of my life. I feel shaky and overwhelmed. This means more than anything I have done. I care so much about acting,' she said, holding the trophy tighter than almost any other winner that night and receiving what fellow nominees said was the loudest and most genuine applause.

Billie then had something else to look forward to – a decent break before having to jump back on to the promotional bandwagon for the start of the second series of *Doctor Who*. She spent her days off finally trying to make her Belsize Park house feel like a home – feeling very aware that she had rarely spent more than a couple of nights at a time there since she had moved in the previous summer.

On the work front, she also had a raft of possible new roles to consider. First up was the part of Sally Bowles in a national tour and West End production of the musical *Cabaret*. The role, made famous by Liza Minnelli in the Oscar-winning film version, would have been a perfect way to combine music and acting. And the Sally Bowles character itself, the louche but lazy nightclub dancer with a hidden heart of gold, was one Billie seemed born to play. But in 2006, it seemed it was a little too early to imagine Billie taking it on. Producers said she would have to give at least a six-month commitment to eight live performances a week and her schedule simply wouldn't allow it.

Billie was also writing in her time off. She got into the habit of jotting down short scenes and even mini-plays when she and Chris had been relaxing in Portugal and

America in their time-out days. Her head, she said, was always buzzing with dramatic ideas and she enjoyed putting many of them down on paper. 'Rightly or wrongly, people see my own life as being dramatic and, instead of looking at that negatively, I can turn it into something positive and find things I can write about in it,' she says. As a lifelong fan of people-watching, she felt she could create some captivating characters as well – people drawn from her travels with Chris, her time on television and film sets, even the regulars in some of her favourite bars.

Amadu's example as a born-again bookworm was also inspiring her to read more and she toyed with the idea of taking a distance learning course in English Literature. More immediately, she made enquiries about doing an intensive six-week course at film school in New York. Her days at acting school in LA when she was married to Chris had been fantastic fun – not least because of the anonymity she enjoyed in America. So learning more about film theory and production on the East Coast seemed equally appealing, although the plan was again put on hold when she realised the odds of her finding a six-week gap in her diary were just about zero.

Having the time to daydream like this in the early spring of 2006 was a rare luxury for Billie. She felt calm, relaxed and, quite simply, happy. Nothing could hurt her, she thought, and nothing could go wrong now her life was on an even keel. So when former *Daily Mirror* editor Piers Morgan got in touch to set up a major interview with *GQ* magazine, she was happy to accept — not least when she found out that David Bailey would be taking the photographs.

The whole thing was all being perfectly timed for the release of the second series of *Doctor Who* in April and Billie decided that there were worse ways to spend an afternoon than doing some high-style photos and chatting with someone as well connected and funny as Piers. Her main portrait for the magazine, a stylish black-and-white shot wearing a black Burberry trench coat, was taken at a studio in London with all the usual crew of make-up and hair-dressers in attendance. With that out of the way, Billie decided to follow the pattern she had set as a teenage pop star. She told her agent she was happy to do the interview on her own. She had never been the kind of prima donna of a star who needs an entourage and a minder around at all times to boost her ego. Or, at least, that was what she thought until she met Piers.

15
LOOSE TALK

BILLIE HAD NEVER met Piers Morgan before, even though he had been a distant friend of Chris's for some 15 years. But the pair got on well from the start – possibly too well, bearing in mind how things turned out. Piers says his biggest initial surprise was that Billie was early – he says he has lost count of the hours he has spent waiting for other celebrities to keep their appointments. And after that, things just kept getting better. 'She looked tiny, but very pretty and has a wonderfully natural smile,' he noted as his first impressions.

The meeting was taking place in the flash but respectable One Aldwych hotel in London's Covent Garden. Billie drank a Diet Coke and two glasses of water – so no one could blame booze for what happened next. But as they talked, Piers soon found out he had a sensation on his hands. 'Whatever you think of Ms Piper, the girl can clearly act… and sing… and has the ability to reduce older men to slavering wrecks. But as we started this interview, I could have no idea, or warning, that it would develop into one of the most extraordinary, revelatory, outrageous and hilarious interviews I have ever done,' Piers wrote in what would be the introduction to his piece.

The *News of the World* certainly agreed. In early April, it got a preview copy of the *GQ* article and printed an edited version of it in a double-page spread under the headline: 'DR WHO STAR BILLIE LAYS BARE HER WILDEST SECRETS. LESBIAN SEX, PORN, QUICKIES AND ME.'

In the article itself, the paper made full use of all the sensationalist capital letters that spice up a great Sunday story. So readers were told:

'We can reveal that Billie LOVES quickie sex. "You just want a quick in and out most times," she said. USES porn to get her going. "I like dirty straight porn," she revealed. FOUND sex a let-down when she first tried it aged just 15. "It couldn't have lasted more than about four minutes." SMOKED cannabis in her "hedonistic" times. LEARNED to be a domestic goddess when she was married to Chris Evans.'

Piers himself admitted that he happily pushed the sexual envelope with some suggestive questions early in the interview. But he says his transcript proves it was Billie who tore right through it. When they got on to the subject of being a sex symbol, and he asked her what she thought her best assets were, it was Billie who offered the extra information that 'I love looking at other women's arses as well.'

'Do you fancy other women?'

'Yeah, big time. I check women out more than I check men out.'

'Have you ever slept with a woman?'

'No.'

'Do you want to?'

'Maybe.'

And so it went on, running through a host of increasingly sexual topics before Piers tried to rein things in.

'What makes you laugh?' he asked.

'People falling over. That always makes me laugh. And Welsh porn.'

'You see, every time I try to change the subject you bring sex back into the interview,' he said.

As the interview unfolded, Billie realised that she had probably said far too much. 'Michael Foster is going to fucking kill me,' she said at one point of her agent's likely reaction. But, somehow, she just seemed to be enjoying herself too much to stop. It felt liberating to be talking so broadly, to be scandalising this man who, in his career as a newspaper editor, had covered every major scandal of the past decade. 'No comment,' might, perhaps, have been the best answer when Piers asked if she had a high sex drive and was a morning or an evening girl. But, for Billie, it didn't feel like a 'no comment' kind of day. So she told it like it is, with 'sometimes' and 'morning' being a rough précis of her much more detailed answers.

The interview and the revelations could well have gone on even longer and got even more X-rated — except for the fact that Piers' Dictaphone ran out of tape. 'Saved by the tape… Oh God, I'm in such trouble. I'm going to have to go home, have a cold shower and lie down. What have I done?' Billie said as they ended the chat and said their goodbyes.

As she left the hotel and headed back to north London, Billie was all too aware that this probably wasn't the end of the story, however. Michael Foster was soon on the phone to find out how the interview had gone and, as Billie had predicted, he was horrified at the subject matters that had been raised. So horrified, in fact, that he rang Piers the following day. 'We have a major problem. You can't put anything in about sex or drugs,' he said. But Piers only laughed. Without those ingredients, there would be nothing left to write up, he told the agent. And so the extraordinary interview was printed up pretty much verbatim in the magazine's May issue and picked up by the *News of the World* and all the other papers.

Hitting the news-stands just as Billie returned to the small screen in what was the BBC's flagship light entertainment show, the revelations could have been career-threatening. No one expected television stars always to act like angels, but there was a strong feeling that they really shouldn't talk like devils. 'It was the kind of interview that would normally trigger the need for some sort of serious damage limitation,' says celebrity PR expert Sophie Coleman. 'Fortunately, three specific points saved Billie's skin. First, and luckily of all, the content was so extreme and was presented in such lurid detail that it seemed unbelievable – people literally dismissed it as exaggeration, if not invention. Second, a close reading showed it was all about Billie's thoughts, not her actions, which kept her one step removed from it. Third, there is the residual affection that people have for Billie, a sense that she has been through the mill already and doesn't deserve any more knocks. People didn't want her career to be affected by a one-off interview. So her best course of action was to pretend it had never happened and thank her lucky stars that she was set to survive it.'

Not that Billie was able to keep out of the public eye. Just as the *GQ* controversy blew up, Billie was revealed as one of the highest climbers in the latest *FHM* World's Sexiest Women poll. She was up 51 places to Number 11, just ahead of the likes of Halle Berry, Jennifer Aniston, Rachel Stevens and Sienna Miller. 'Billie has taken everybody by surprise. The last time we looked, she was a toothy bundle of hair in a pub garden with Chris Evans. Now she is a gorgeous, prime-time goddess with her own action figure,' said editor Ross Brown, who had clearly missed some of the more recent glamour shots of the star.

Flattered by the compliments and the comparisons but still embarrassed by her *GQ* moment, Billie couldn't wait to get the focus back on her acting, and she was soon going to get the chance. The small matter of the screening of the second series of *Doctor Who* was looming and Billie headed back to Cardiff for the big press launch. This year's extravaganza was held at the city's extraordinary Millennium Centre which had been used as a location for much of the first episode of the series. Once again, several hundred newspaper, magazine and television reporters were there and, once again, Billie was the centre of attention.

She wore a casual, pale-brown and sometimes almost see-through top and smiled widely as she enthused about the new episodes, the new Doctor and her new-found notoriety. Fortunately for her, and for everyone concerned with the show, Billie's new 'nation's sweetheart' status hadn't been jeopardised by her loose talk. As Sophie Coleman had predicted, children had ignored it, and adults had taken it in their stride. 'Our Billie' wasn't going to be thrown out of the national soap opera quite so easily.

Doctor Who fever was also in full swing. The *Radio Times* produced a fantastic fold-out cover for the edition previewing the new series (copies of it became collectors' items, attracting dozens of bids and selling for many times the original cover price on auction sites such as ebay). And when the first episode, 'New Earth', was finally broadcast on Saturday, 15 April 2006, some 8.6

million viewers tuned in. That was nearly two million less than the first episode of the previous series, but this time around David and Rose had been up against a *Harry Potter* film on ITV and it still managed to be the most popular show of the week once *Coronation Street* and *EastEnders* were taken out of the equation.

It also seemed as if everyone liked what they saw. The ratings rose the following week, with 9.24 million tuning in for the far darker 'Tooth and Claw', which had Pauline Collins playing Queen Victoria, Billie's Rose trying desperately to use the phrase 'we are not amused' and some brilliantly realistic and terrifying monsters changing form and racing at all the good guys. Viewers were so gripped by the show that even *Doctor Who Confidential*, the behind-the-scenes programme on BBC Three, beat audience records for its channel as well.

There were, of course, some who wanted to opt out of *Doctor Who* or Billie mania. Tom Cox, reviewing the week's television for the *Mail on Sunday*, was one of them. He wasn't particularly impressed by the show, by David Tennant or, least of all, Billie Piper. 'BILLIE'S A WASTE OF TIME,' ran the headline, and the article itself confirmed his view. 'The sub-Eccleston Tennant was OK, in the way that Gabriel Byrne is OK when a director can't afford Al Pacino,' Cox began. 'But it was all too easy to overlook his pleasantly manic presence as Piper trampled all over it with some of the worst diction since the last series of *Big Brother*. It's not just that Piper is given too much room here, or even that she is beginning to look more and more like Bingo, the gorilla from the Banana Splits, it's also that every time she's on camera she radiates the aura of someone who believes they are two or three times more good looking and talented than they actually are. When she held up a large, mysterious diamond, it was hard not to picture a GCSE drama teacher standing next to her saying, "You have just been handed a large, mysterious diamond – please show us how you would look at it."'

Other mild sniping was surprisingly rare, however, and by the time summer approached, the series had bedded down nicely and the vast majority of other critics were continuing to lavish praise on the series and almost all its main actors. There was a real sense that the show was getting better and better, in the writing, the production, the performances – the whole expensive package.

Having the Cybermen return in the fifth and sixth episodes was another triumph. Exactly 40 years after their first appearance in the show, the Cybermen had been given what was described as a 'new futuristic-retro' look. Led by Roger Lloyd Pack (Trigger from *Only Fools and Horses*), they enjoyed a high-profile double bill and expectations of it were so high that Cardiff-born *Blue Peter* presenter Gethin Jones accepted a role as one of them, even though he would be completely unidentifiable in his costume.

The two episodes gave Billie some more emotional depth to play as she tried to see through the parallel universe to contact her parents. As usual, the writers had also decided to make Billie the butt of some light-hearted jokes – in the parallel universe, there would still be a character called Rose, for example, but after teasing the viewers by keeping the new Rose off camera for half the show, she was introduced not as a feisty early 20-something woman but as a tiny, yappy little lap-dog. Raising her famous eyebrows at the writers as she read her script, Billie was the first to admit that she saw the joke. Eventually.

16
MOVING ON

SO WHY WOULD you leave such an obvious hit show? As summer approached, the rumours intensified that Billie wasn't in the latter episodes of the second series (totally untrue, as viewers would soon find out) and that she was ultimately going to leave the show. Actress Eve Myles was named as her most likely replacement, after winning a big role in the spin-off show *Torchwood*. Then there was talk that the Doctor might get his first male assistant, with Noel Clarke's Mickey Smith touted as the most likely candidate.

Most interesting of all came the rumour that Billie might stay with the show but with a slight promotion – if change was in the air, could she be the first female Doctor? While David Tennant did say he was so happy in the role that he could imagine doing it for decades, the idea of Billie one day guiding the TARDIS wasn't officially denied by the producers. Watch this space (or, more accurately, watch space) the fans were told.

The final threat to Billie's role was a worry that having proved herself both a superb actress and a huge ratings draw, a rival channel such as ITV might make her the kind of financial and creative offer no one would be able to refuse. The channel had already approached her about playing the role of Fanny Price in a big budget re-make of Jane Austin's *Mansfield Park*, something Billie was hugely attracted to doing if she could only find the time. 'We want the absolute cream of British acting talent,' ITV Drama Director Nick Elliott said as the first approaches were made to Billie. But she remained unsure if she could or should accept the offer.

'This was clearly going to be a very important and difficult time for Billie,' says showbusiness agent Stella Martin. 'Actors often feel a knee-jerk fear of being typecast, which is often misplaced. And in a show such as *Doctor Who*, the concept of being typecast is actually a little bit false. Yes, you play the same character every week, but the scripts mean you also get to try your hand at comedy, drama and action. As the settings around you change, from pre-revolutionary France to the Second World War to the extreme future, you also get to adapt your style accordingly. So it should be possible to stay in the same role and still enjoy a lot of creative freedom.'

Stella also warned against Billie accepting a huge new 'golden handcuffs' deal with a rival channel. 'The problem with these is that you are tied to the channel even before suitable roles for you have been written. Several former soap stars who claimed they wanted to escape the typecasting trap then found themselves doing one big-budget drama after another where they simply seemed to play the same SAS agent, rogue cop or tragic mother. If you really want to stretch yourself as an actor, you are probably better off choosing each role individually rather than signing up to a huge deal and then hoping that the right jobs come in.'

Fortunately for Billie, the BBC was well aware of her talent and was keen to give her plenty to do in the *Doctor Who* off-season. It had bought the rights to the quartet of Philip Pullman novels featuring the Victorian sleuth Sally Lockhart. 'They are historical thrillers, good old-fashioned, blood–and-thunder melodramas,' says the author, and the central role in them seemed tailor-made for Billie. The Corporation got in touch and talked Billie through their plans for the first of the adaptations, *The Ruby in the Smoke*, and its follow-up, *The Shadow in the North*. Both were being written for television by Adrian Hodges, the writer behind *Rome*, who had a fantastic reputation for strong characterisations. Billie was entranced and thrilled. Sally Lockhart was exactly the kind of high-profile new role she could only have dreamed of winning just over two years earlier, when most of her early auditions seemed to end in failure. It was exactly what she had been hoping for when she took her acting classes high in the

Hollywood Hills back in 2003. Everyone agreed. 'Billie is an extremely versatile actress and the perfect choice for bringing to life this engaging and fearless heroine,' said BBC Head of Drama Serials Laura Mackie after the contracts were signed.

The show is set in Victorian London and this kind of period role was another new stretch for Billie — which she said was another good reason for agreeing to it. Acting alongside co-stars such as Julie Waters was another big draw. The one factor which didn't sway Billie's decision was the money, though the deal her agent struck was one of the best in television drama at an estimated £90,000 per adaptation.

Ever since her childhood, Billie had been determined to stand on her own two feet financially. She hadn't been able to access all the cash she had earned from her first commercials and even her early music money was held in trust until she reached 18. But all along, it had meant a great deal to her to know that funds were building up in the background, to be withdrawn later should they be required. The girl who had started off wanting to be free of suburban Swindon grew to place just as much value on financial freedom.

'Having some money means I don't have to let that subject dictate the roles that I choose,' she said. 'I don't have to do things for the sake of them and I know I am very lucky in that. It means I can wait a while and find the right things. I've had the time to go out and find out about life, to observe people and dynamic situations that help me in my work. Ultimately, I am only ever going to do the things that interest me and that I feel I can do something with. If that means people don't see the work, then that doesn't really bother me. I need to be part of things that make me feel alive. Even if I am offered a blockbuster, it may not be right at the time or benefit me enough for me to agree to it.'

Filming for *The Ruby in the Smoke* began in London in May 2006 – and was immediately interrupted by one fantastic event. It was Bafta time in London and *Doctor Who* looked like being a big winner. The event, the British Academy of Film and Television Awards, was the most well-established and prestigious of the burgeoning celebrity circuit with everyone from Laurence Olivier to Judi Dench among the alumni. If *Doctor Who* won any of the big awards, then Billie had been picked by the crew to collect them.

As usual, she was nervous. Every time she attended an awards ceremony, her mind went back to the humiliation of being booed off stage by 5ive fans when she had won accolades as a singer. But in May 2006, there was no chance of this happening in the ballroom of London's Grosvenor House Hotel. *Doctor Who* was a popular winner of the viewer-voted Pioneer Audience Award and the Bafta Best Drama Serial. And Billie was a hugely popular person to be welcomed on to the stage. After kissing a kilted David Tennant, who was sitting to her left on the *Doctor Who* table, Billie wound her way to the podium amidst uninterrupted applause.

'This is such a treat. Thank you. Thank you so much,' she said, her wide smile looking even brighter than normal.

Back at her table, Billie was as gripped as everyone else when the Best Actress category was announced. *Bleak House* co-stars Gillian Anderson and Anna Maxwell Martin were nominated alongside Anne-Marie Duff from *Shameless* and Lucy Cohu from Channel Four's *The Queen's Sisters*. In the end, Anna Maxwell Martin won the award and Billie applauded with everyone else as the actress took to the stage and made her brief acceptance speech. Could Billie be nominated in the same category next year, or soon after that? Few people would have put money on her getting this far when she was dismissed as a drunken former pop star with more money than sense. So the odds of her achieving this next goal suddenly seemed a great deal shorter.

As summer came – and after *Things to Do Before You're 30* pretty much sank without trace in the cinemas – there was also talk that Hollywood might be calling. Billie said she dreamt of being in a Mike Leigh or Woody Allen film, but not everyone thought she should go to America – or at least not yet. Pete Bowker, the writer on *The Canterbury Tales* who had been one of Billie's earliest supporters, said she might be wasted in the American system. 'I don't know that Hollywood quite understands how attractive Billie is and her look. And she isn't the kind of person who would go to LA to hang around to get the odd role in the hope of getting a really good part one day. She is someone who needs to be working and needs to be doing interesting stuff.'

Even if she did head west, Billie found that she couldn't rely on *Doctor Who* to be her automatic calling card for Hollywood. The show was being broadcast on the Sci-Fi Channel just after the equally big-budget American remake of *Battlestar Galactica*. But while *Battlestar* was attracting decent audiences in the States, the ratings charts showed a quarter of the viewers turned off when *Doctor Who* came on. In what was dubbed 'the battle of the sci-fi babes', 23-year-old Billie was said to be losing out badly to 32-year-old *Battlestar* actress Tricia Helfer.

For Billie, though, the competition was already over. She had decided to take a break from *Doctor Who* – though no-one was ruling out a return at some point in the future.

'Rose and I have gone on the most incredible journey over the past two years and I can confirm it has come to an end, for now at least,' she said, as fans prepared for the end of series finale which would reveal her dramatic exit.

She revealed in an interview with the *Radio Times* that her decision to leave the hit programme had been difficult, adding: 'The longer I stayed, the more scared I'd be of leaving. I'm utterly grateful for the whole experience but you have to take care of yourself and do what you feel is right.'

A new assistant would indeed travel with David Tennant in 2007. But however gruesome Rose's exit was to be, the door would stay open should Billie ever want to reboard the TARDIS. 'No-one ever stays dead in science fiction,' joked *SFX* magazine editor Dave Bradley, saying fans would always welcome Billie back into the show.

In the meantime the girl who had spent so much of her life in a hurry was finally ready to slow down. She wanted to take some time off to travel, and as she planned a trip to India and Africa she realised she had found the one thing her life had so often lacked: serenity. 'I'm not in it for the fame or money,' she said of her new career and mental outlook. 'I'm in the business because I love it and that's a really reassuring thought. Now I just have to do what I want to do. I used to feel the pressure of it all. Maybe I should do this, because last time I did that. They criticised me for "x, y and z" so maybe I should do "a, b and c". Finally, I've got to the point where I have stopped caring about all that. I just do what I do and I'm loving it.'

As if to emphasise her new sense of wellbeing, in a shockingly frank interview with the *Radio Times* in the summer of 2006 the increasingly mature Billie revealed that she had in fact dabbled in drugs and drink as an overwhelmed teenager. She even confessed that at the age of 16 she had endured a 'very dark moment… when I didn't want to be here any more – but I did nothing about it, thank God.

'I was saved mostly by my parents, friends and boyfriends, but it could have gone either way.'

But Billie was proud that, despite her hugely eventful

life, she was able to put her hand on her heart and say she had no regrets over any of the things she had done, or any of the turns she had taken. She has hit the top in two fiercely competitive professions. She has broken old records and set new ones. She has found love, lost it, and yet still kept it alive. She has explored her own ambitions and ultimately discovered her own peace of mind.

In 2006, her life had, in some ways, gone full circle back to a night in February 2001 when she had first started dating Chris Evans. On the evening in question, Billie had left an Indian restaurant in Notting Hill with a huge smile on her face.

'What are you celebrating?' the waiter asked her, intrigued.

'Life. I'm just celebrating life,' she shouted back at him, with an even wider smile.

A lot has gone wrong in Billie's life since that February night, but even more has gone right. Today, she has finally started to celebrate all over again.